FROM POM POMS TO PRISON

SUSAN DeFACE WASHINGTON

Copyright © 2015 by Susan DeFace Washington.
All rights reserved.

ISBN: 978-1-5086-3405-8

From Pom Poms to Prison published by Triumph Press

Backcover photography: Jennifer Bernal Photography

info@TriumphPress.com

No part of this book may be reproduced or transmitted in any form or by any means, electronic or mechanical, including scanning, photocopying, recording, or by any information storage and retrieval system, without permission in writing from the publisher.

10 9 8 7 6 5 4 3 2 1

Other Books by Triumph Press

★ ★ ★

The Triumph Book by Melanie Davis

The Triumph Book: HEROES by Melanie Davis and 27 Veterans

The Triumph Program by Melanie Davis

The Triumph Program: Military Edition by Melanie Davis and Matthew Brown USMC

Healing the Warrior Heart: A Glimpse into the Hearts of Combat Veterans and their Supporting Loved Ones by Andrew R. Jones USMC Combat Veteran

A Combat Nightmare in WWII by LTC Julian A Roadman

Fully Prepped? by Todd Jones

My Brother in Arms: The Exceptional Life of Mark Andrew Forester, United States Air Force Combat Controller by Thad Forester

Triumph Press is a resource for those who have the passion to tell their life-stories and change the world. If you have a true and inspiring story to share, visit *www.TriumphPress.com* to learn how we can help you publish and join our library of inspirational books.

I would like to dedicate my book to my children and husband: Hailey, Sammy, Alexis, Riley, and Warner.

Praise for Susan Washington and her Story

Reading this book brought tears to my eyes many times. Through sadness and sometimes rage with those around her who could have helped and didn't, I have come to a peaceful and joyful place in my heart for Susan. I know she is and will continue to fulfill the promise of her fabulous brain, talent, humor and potential through her compulsion to be kind and helpful, her hard-won faith and her God-given strength.
  – **Peri Gilpin**, *Susan's longtime friend and who played the character, Roz, from the sitcom Frasier*

I had the opportunity to interview Susan on my Renewal Radio program. I'm totally impressed with her story. In fact, it's hard to believe. It's a story of God's grace in a way that is almost unbelievable. How Susie survived all of the abuse is beyond my own comprehension. As she unfolded her story, I frankly was emotionally impacted in ways that normally does not happen. My producer and engineer felt the very same way.

– **Dr. Gene Getz**- *Renewal Radio-graduate of Moody Bible Institute, Author of more than fifty books. Currently, Gene serves as a senior pastor of Fellowship Bible Church North in Plano, Texas; director of the Center for Church Renewal; host of Renewal Radio; and adjunct professor at Dallas Theological Seminary*

Susan DeFace Washington has one of the most powerful stories of redemption I've ever heard. Her story combined with her heart to help others experience the freedom she has found is unmatched. If you ever meet Susan you will know two things immediately: 1. She is a changed person and 2. She cares deeply. Susan has a way of sharing that disarms the hardest cynic with hilarious transparency and blunt truth about life, choices, and the love of God.

– **Keith Spurgin,** *Lead Pastor of New Hope Christian Church-Wylie Texas*

From tragic to triumphant! Susan DeFace Washington is living proof of God's grace, mercy and love. Her zeal joined with humility, compassion, grace and love....and patience/persistence is heartwarming and inspiring.

– **Joe Shearin,** *currently in private practice in Dallas, Texas, as a highly rated criminal defense attorney and former NFL football player for the Los Angeles Rams, Tampa Bay Buccaneers, and the Dallas Cowboys*

In 2003, after being paroled, Susan's conversion began when she met a family who lost their child to a tragic accident. They, Susan observed, had not fallen apart but had turned to God and allowed his mercy and strength to help them through. Susan from that day forward surrendered her life to Jesus Christ.

– **Kristie Smith.** *"God Never Gave Up on One Fallen Educator." Dallas Morning News 20 Jan 2012*

When you speak or read about Susan you truly get the meaning of don't ever, ever give up. She shows us all that anything is possible through faith!

– **Manuel Flores**

"She served a year in prison, sharing a dorm with one woman who had decapitated her parents and one who had microwaved her baby."

– *"Wylie Woman Inspires by Sharing Tragic Past." Wylie News 14 Jan 2012*

Susan, you have been such a blessing to the HOPE women and we are excited about having you speak to them again. I am thrilled about what God is going to do to minister to many incarcerated women. They hunger for people who understand the struggles of incarceration and separation from family. Your testimony will bring a message of hope and freedom to them, and the power of God's amazing grace to redeem and restore.

– **Lucy Smith,** *MEd, QI, CALT- Hope Literacy TDCJ*

From what I have observed, Susan's story deeply affects those who read it. Her honesty, transparency, and wit are testimonies to God's true and abiding presence in her life. From her pain, we see beauty. From her beauty, truth. From her truth, life. Something that these days, amidst all the noise and pain in our world, is desperately needed.

– **Lisa Johnson,** *Emmy Award-Winning Writer and Filmmaker and Co-Director/Producer of "His Name is Bob."*

"Washington . . travels across Dallas-Fort Worth to tell the tale of a Dallas girl with a difficult home life who later turned to drug abuse as an adult and ultimately went to prison. But now, she said, her Christian faith has helped her to turn her life around — and to open up. She speaks at churches, schools and even the rehabilitation center where she was sent after her first indictment. At each one, her goal is the same: to tell her story and encourage others to tell theirs."

– **Haesemeyer, Ruth.** *"Into the Light: Susan DeFace Washington of Wylie Looking to Share Story of Grief, Struggles, Hope." (The Dallas Morning News) Feb 2012*

Susan, I'm so glad that you are using your experience to help people. I could tell my kids all of the things you might tell them; but your experience gives that message a credibility I could never give it.

– **Joe Baker**

Your story has been a gift to my life. I have no doubt you will touch many lives that are lost, and God will use you to gently guide them back. I am thankful for the blessing of your acquaintance. You are an AMAZING woman!

– **Tammy Forrester Bowman**

I have had the opportunity to hear Susan DeFace Washington speak on more than one occasion. After hearing her story, all I could think was that it was one of the most courageous testimonies I have ever heard. She is living proof of God's power and grace.

– **Randy Smith,** *Sunday School teacher at First Baptist Church of Allen*

Even though I am only 11 years old, I have read a couple of parts of the book and I've been touched by it! When my mom buys the book I'm going to read it with her every night because I think it is beautiful!

– **Micah Tanner Mann**

Susan's story will keep you wanting more. More faith, hope, love and the same support system that she has found through Jesus Christ. It takes you through her dark times which will definitely hit home even if your problems are not exactly the same. Best of all, it takes you through the ups and downs of her recovery and details the journey of what has got her through to where she is today. It is encouraging and uplifting. If you or someone you know is struggling with addiction you do not want to miss this opportunity. It could change your life, it did mine!

– **Rebecca Burns**

I interviewed Susan DeFace Washington for The Wylie News and couldn't believe my ears as she told me all the things she'd been through. Not only had she survived experiences that would've sent me cowering under my bed, she had learned from her mistakes and come out on the other side eager to tell her story, one she calls 'a story of hope.' She was very inspirational to me, and I was honored to write about her.

– **Judy Truesdell**, *Staff Writer, C&S Media*

Susan's story of heartbreak, perseverance, courage, redemption and hope is one that touches me deeply. Knowing the beautiful, intelligent cheerleader from high school, one would never suspect her home was filled with sadness and solitude.

– **Lori Stephenson**

I don't know one person whose life has not been affected by some sort of addiction. I believe your story has and can continue to help so many who have been affected. I wish you the best of luck and hope to be able to purchase a copy of your book soon.

– **Susan Martin Estrella**

Susan, your transparency is such a gift. Your stories are heart-wrenching and inspirational. And your willingness to share them is bound to transform lives. Thank you for being a catalyst for so many others that will follow after you.

– **Lisa Jenkins Watson**

Susan knows what it is to lose everything, including her dignity, and by losing the world she gained her soul and God's glory of eternity. God loved her when she was unlovable, gave her a new heart, and sent her on a mission to tell the world of his love and power.

– **Michael McCullough**

She is already making a difference by helping so many that have reached out to her in need of faith and guidance.

– Melanie Ellis

Susan's story is one of tragedy, like so many others, but the incredible difference is how Susan changed the trajectory of her life into one with such a bright future. It's been amazing to watch the transformation in Susan's life. Susan's story is one of powerful transformation and redemption. It will encourage you and give you hope that you can truly overcome life's greatest struggles and tragedies. You can find purpose and meaning behind your past hurts and use them to help others and make the world a better place.

– **Dan and Kerri Jensen** –*parents of Alex Jensen who died tragically in a snow skiing accident at the age of 12. God used this tragedy for good as he so often does. Countless people have come to know the Lord through Alex's death and Susan was one of them.*

Susan - Your presentation to our 5th grade students last week was outstanding and emotional. I've never seen our students so captivated by a speaker, as they were with you. They seemed to connect with you. I believe that listening to your story really made a difference in their lives. You reaffirmed that it's all about choices. The teachers were commenting all day, what a great speech you gave to our students. Thank you so much!

– **Yvette Yanez Brown**- *Counselor at Gilbert Elementary*

Susan, I think back to February 13 when we met you and I know that God had a hand in all of that. I also know that her recovery is, in part, due to you and your prayer warriors. God put you here to help people and that's exactly what you're doing. Thank you for everything and for your continued prayers!

    – **Paula Stephenson,** *friend (Susan reached out to her daughter who was addicted to Meth and she is now clean.)*

My Prayer for You

As I look back on my life, the good and the bad, I can see God everywhere. His hand was always on my life, softening the blows that didn't deserve to be softened.

My life is full of many tragic sorrows; some that were out of my control and others that were a consequence of my bad choices. It is amazing to look back and see how God protected me.

I praise my Savior because I surely did not deserve his protection. But He loved me and never gave up. I am so thankful to Him that I feel I have been led to write and share my testimony, which brings glory to God.

He has restored me and taught me what is truly important in this life. He gently admonishes me and shows me the error in my thinking. Our thoughts are so important, and the origins of our thoughts are essential to know.

There is an enemy in this world ready to devour and ruin our lives. All he wants is to steal our peace and rob us of eternal life with our Heavenly Father. We must be on our guard and in constant communication with Jesus to prevent that from happening. If we take our eyes off Jesus, it is so easy to slip.

My prayer for you is to have an intimate relationship with God and to understand that this relationship will bring you all that you have been longing for. For years I tried to fill the empty hole inside me with drugs, alcohol, material possessions, and many other destructive behaviors. These worked for a while, but then they took over my life and brought about destruction.

Only by the grace of God was I not destroyed; I came close, but He has restored my life. I will share my experiences in hopes that it will help you.

God is the way and the truth; John 8:31-32 "If you abide in my word you are my disciples indeed. And you shall know the truth and the truth shall make your free." That sums it all up: when we live in sin, we are in the dark, hiding who we really are; but if we step out in faith and become open and transparent, there will be no darkness and the truth will free us from the bondage that has trapped us.

—Susan DeFace Washington

Table of Contents

Prologue 17

It Is Such A Secret Place 21

Loneliness Is Not What It Seems 27

The Secret I've Kept Locked Away,
No One Can Ever See 37

You Think You Have A Memory, But It Has You 49

It's A Slow Fade... 55

The Darkest Hour Comes Before The Dawn 65

Sometimes What Seems Like Surrender Isn't
Surrender At All 89

Walk Awhile In My Shoes 111

Beautiful People Do Not Just Happen 123

Without The Struggle, The Butterfly Would Never,
Ever Fly 137

Mercies In Disguise 153

Prologue

People are like stained glass windows. They sparkle and shine when the sun is out, but when the darkness sets in, their beauty is revealed only if there is a light from within.
— Elisabeth Kübler-Ross

My name is Susan and I was born in Dallas, Texas on December 19th, 1960. I was the youngest of three children. My sister Kathey was ten years older than me and my brother David was eight years older.

My mother's name was Rosemary and she was a stay-at-home mom while my father, Richard, had two salvage stores that he owned in Dallas and nearby Balch Springs. My grandfather on my mother's side gave him these stores after the company he worked for, Mobil Oil, was going to transfer him to New York City.

As far as I can remember I think we were an average family, other than the fact that both my sister and brother were profoundly hearing impaired. They were born hearing but, when they were about three years old, they lost most of their ability to hear. To this day, the cause of the hearing loss is unclear but different theories have been bounced around through the years, from some genetic disability to childhood vaccinations. It was even theorized to have been a form of penicillin called streptomycin they received when they were ill. While we were never certain of the cause, the genetic disability was dismissed after I was born and never experienced a hearing loss. The anguish this must have put upon my parents is incomprehensible. I am not sure what affect it had on them but it must have been devastating for your two children to hear fine one day and be profoundly deaf the next. They must have carried a lot of guilt playing the "what if" and "if only" games in their minds. The thought that they may have caused this or could have prevented it in some way must have tormented them.

Kathey and David attended regular public schools as well as Stonewall Jackson Elementary. Stonewall had a program for the hearing impaired and served as the area's Regional School for the Deaf. In spite of their hearing loss, they were both very intelligent. Kathey excelled in school, graduating at the top of her class of 1200 at Bryan Adams High School in 1968. She received a full academic scholarship to Southern Methodist University. David, on the other hand, was also very intelligent but not as academically successful; a contention between him and my father.

In hindsight, we certainly fit the stereotypical roles in a dysfunctional family with the oldest child being the hero, the middle being the scapegoat, and the youngest being the mascot and peacekeeper. I wasn't sure why we were dysfunctional at that time but these roles were well defined with Kathey, David, and I playing out our parts all too well.

I don't really recall my younger years with much clarity, except for small fragments that seem to flash into my mind at unexpected times. My memories before the age of ten remind me of a pinball machine: bing bing bing, Christmas mornings, pow pow, snow skiing in New Mexico in the winter and spring, bump bum, the lake house, ca-chunk, water skiing, ratatatat, diving lessons in Galveston and, buzzzz, kickball games in the alley are the way these memories surface. They pop up and flash randomly without warning, bouncing around like an arcade game in my head.

While there is never an order to these memories, and at times I don't know what triggers them, they always bring a smile to my face. They remind me of a time when life must have been somewhat simple and happy for my family. A time before the destruction and dysfunction invaded our home, bringing a cloud of darkness that would cover my life for decades.

My Family

Momma , Kathey, and David probably 1954

Momma in happier times.

CHAPTER 1

It Is Such A Secret Place

It is such a secret place, the land of tears.
— Antoine de Saint-Exupery

In 1971, the summer began with life being carefree and fun. We spent most of the time at our lake house on Cedar Creek Lake, about an hour's drive from Dallas. David had just graduated from Woodrow Wilson High School and Kathey was finishing her second year at SMU.

Looking back, I was very excited about that Fourth of July. We were planning to shoot fireworks off the pier and into the lake. My parents and I were already settled in at the lake house and we were waiting for Kathey and David's arrival. I wasn't allowed to shoot off any fireworks until David got there. Being only 10 years old, the day seemed to drag by slowly as I anticipated his arrival. To pass the time, I wanted to go waterskiing. Norman and Barbara agreed to indulge me.

Norman, my dad's best friend, was driving the boat and his wife, Barbara, was going to ski with me. My parents had met Norman and Barbara a few years before and they had become best friends. They had a lake house next door to ours and we spent a lot of time with their family. It felt good to be in the water; it was cool on my legs. The ski was heavy as I tried to control it before Norman pulled the slack from the rope. As we were getting ready to speed off, I noticed a man walking down our pier. His posture seemed off because his head was hanging down.

This man was only an acquaintance of my parents so it was unusual for him to visit us. He had the only house with a telephone in our subdivision at the lake. The man leaned down and said something to my mother that was so bad she collapsed and had to be carried off the pier. We stopped the boat; and I got out of the water. No one would talk to or tell me what was going on. I still don't remember how I found out, but I did. That day I was too scared to ask what had happened and there was a voice inside telling me I would be better off not knowing the truth. The truth was my brother had committed suicide. He shot himself. David had shut the door to his bedroom and fired the gun into his mouth. After David's suicide everything in my family changed.

July 4th, 1971, is my first memory. It is the first "day" I really remember; parts of it are still so vivid in my mind. My parents were in such pain they both turned to alcohol. They had always drank, but now it was much more and every day.

The year after David died, another tragedy struck my family. My dad's best friend, Norman, went to my dad's store to see him. My father was very busy and asked Norman if they could talk later. Norman went to my dad's truck and took his gun. He drove to White Rock Lake, parked the car, and shot himself, just like David. He was a pharmaceutical salesman and had been caught stealing. I guess he couldn't face the consequences of his actions and chose to end his life. This was another blow to our family. After his suicide, my dad parked Norman's car in our driveway. I remember peeking into the window of that car and looking at the bloodstained seats. I don't know why he kept that car in our driveway where our family and all of the neighborhood children could see it. It is still such a haunting memory.

This is what my life looked like. My dad dealt with his overwhelming grief by going out to bars and drinking. My mother only drank at home. My sister was away at college. I spent most of my time alone. It was now normal for me to be by myself. This is just the way it was. I think I was happy because I really didn't know any differently. My parent's alcoholism was progressing substantially, with my mother's reaching new heights.

The years after David's death, I don't know what I thought my mother's problem was. As her alcoholism advanced, her ability to hide it became harder. When I was in eighth grade, I finally figured it out. The school I attended, J.L. Long Jr. High, was quite a distance from my home and I was involved in many extracurricular activities. I remember waiting at the school or at the YMCA for my mother to pick me up. She never came. To this day I can still feel the painful knot in my stomach, eating away at me, as I stood on the curb looking for her car that would never arrive. It was so very unnerving because I just didn't understand what was happening to my family. I'd have to find a ride with someone else which was embarrassing to me. When I would arrive home, she would be "asleep" and I would not be able to wake her up. I was so scared that I usually would just go to my room, turn on my TV, or my record player to escape the silence and loneliness that was consuming me. I would wait anxiously for my Dad to come home, which was usually very late. Finally, I decided to investigate and see what was going on. As I searched through the house, I found containers of Vodka stashed away in various places. I now suspected she had a drinking problem, but didn't know what to do to help her. I didn't want to share this with anyone. I didn't know any other parents who were alcoholics. The best way to deal with this, I thought, was to pretend everything was fine. That everything was normal.

The façade I created to the outside world was very believable and not many people knew about my home life. I did well in school, was popular among my peers, but deep down inside I was in an enormous amount of pain. During my junior high year, I started drinking, as did many of my friends. I didn't become dependent on alcohol but, if I drank, I drank to get drunk. Many kids were using marijuana at this time and although I did try it; I didn't like it. The idea of drugs was dangerous to me, so I just stuck with alcohol. Junior High School was when the fear began to grow because my mother slept more and more and my father stayed out later and later.

Cheering at a football game.
Cheerleading brought me a lot of joy.

J.L Long Junior High with friends

My brother's senior portrait taken just
a few months before he took his life.

CHAPTER 2
Loneliness Is Not What It Seems

Loneliness is not what it seems. One does not feel lonely because one is alone, but because of a feeling of lack - a feeling that something is missing. Loneliness is essentially independent of how many other humans are around.
— *Jonathan Lockwood Huie*

As I entered high school, my home life got worse. My mother's drinking was beyond out of control. I came home from school one day to find empty perfume and cologne bottles scattered all over the house. I couldn't figure out what had happened or what was going on.

As was customary, my mother was passed out on the floor. As I bent down to check on her, I could smell the sweetness on her breath. It was Grey Flannel, a popular men's cologne at the time. To this day, that smell repulses me. She had run out of vodka, so she drank anything with alcohol in it. This time it was perfume and cologne; the only things she could find readily available; other times it was rubbing alcohol, Nyquil, or mouthwash. When she couldn't find alcohol, she would start to withdraw and experience the delirium tremens or DTs. This form of crashing would cause hallucinations and can lead to death. When she did this, I would have to take her to the hospital to detox. She would get out of the hospital only to begin drinking again and the cycle would start over. This happened more frequently as the years went on. Each time I was there for her.

One time I remember she ran out of the house with just a bathrobe on, screaming and crying about spiders attacking her. She was swatting in the air at the imaginary spiders. I chased her around our house to the back and was able to bring her inside without any of the neighbors seeing her. It was such a lonely, scary time for me. I am still amazed that I could keep all this sadness and fear hidden at school, and from my schoolmates

Although there was such extreme neglect and dysfunction in my home - there was money. Money, however, made it more confusing to me because, in a way, it made me feel privileged: I got a car when I turned sixteen; I had a closet full of new clothes; and I had cash with me every day. I could always buy whatever I wanted and I did. Shopping was my way to get out of the house and buying myself new things made me feel better, easing the extreme pain, albeit momentarily.

As I have said, school was very enjoyable for me. It was an escape from the pain of my home life; however, I certainly made some poor choices, especially where dating was concerned. At the beginning of my sophomore year, I met a boy that seemed very special. He had beautiful red hair with golden highlights and was so incredibly funny. His sense of humor was amazing and it wasn't long before Allen and I became an "item," dating exclusively. There were lots of laughs and crazy stunts. We could be so silly. .. and silly felt good.

My best friend, Peri, had gotten a job at Taco Bueno. At orientation, she had to sign an affidavit promising never to disclose the recipe for the guacamole dip. Allen and I thought that was hilarious. One night, when she was getting off work, we disguised ourselves in trench coats and sunglasses; and we were driving a car she wouldn't recognize. We waited outside the employee exit. When she emerged, we "kidnapped" her, demanding the recipe. Peri and I still laugh about that to this day. Although there was a lot of fun in this relationship, it turned extremely abusive, very quickly.

I don't really remember when the hitting began. I'm somewhat surprised that I don't remember the first time it happened, but at some point it became routine and quickly a part of our relationship. I just don't know how. The neglect and abuse were becoming more extreme at home, but it was never physical. My father was verbally abusive and my mother was just absent, so it still shocks me on some level that I tolerated this different kind of abuse. Although my special boy and I had a lot of fun, our relationship was built on a lot of drinking. I know that played a huge factor in the abuse that took place.

One of the worst bouts of physical abuse happened when we were at a club (don't ask me how we went to clubs in high school but we did.). It was a club called PT's on Lawther Drive, off Northwest Highway near White Rock Lake. (It had been a strip club once, but wasn't then.) We were with a lot of kids from school when Allen and I got into a fight. This fight lead to our break-up that night and he began to make-out with another girl in a booth. To get back at him, I decided to dance with a boy who had always had a crush on me. Just after we started to dance, Allen came over, pushed Billy out of the way, grabbed me, and bit through my cheek. It was bad. I was bleeding and people jumped up to separate us. Everyone there just chalked it up to too much alcohol, but I knew differently. This had happened before, but never in front of people. In the past, Allen was always careful to hit me where the bruises would not be visible. An older boy I knew named Keith and his date gave me a ride home. By the time we left the club, my face was swollen and bruised from the bite. Keith's date asked me what on earth I would tell my parents. I just remember looking at her and saying, "I'll be able to conceal it." I knew that my parents would never notice because my dad didn't live in the home anymore; and my mother was never coherent. Inside, I knew I only had to hide the bruises from my friends and people at school. I remember sitting in the backseat of her green cougar, gazing out the window, absent-mindedly brushing my fingers across the bite mark, feeling such shame.

I can't recall what would set off his anger, but Allen would just explode. One time we were at White Rock Lake and he was driving my car. He got so angry that he grabbed my head with one hand and held it in his lap, then began pummeling me with his fist. I tried hard to get away, but couldn't. I was scared that this time he would really hurt me. I finally grabbed my gear shift and threw the car in park. This made him let go of me and slow down. I jumped out of the car and began to run for my life. He was very careful to only hit my head, and not my face. I remember my head being so sore, but there were no visible bruises. He was very skilled at this kind of abuse.

Of course, Allen would always apologize and promise to never do it again, proclaiming his love for me. Then he would make me laugh and I would forgive him, believing that that would be the last time. Maybe I was so desperate for love that I continued to take this abuse, I don't know. Allen had some wonderful qualities, but the bottom line is he abused me horribly.

As time went on, the abuse got more violent and I felt our relationship was nearing its end. We kept breaking up and getting back together. He was so terribly controlling that I was isolated from my friends. He even talked me out of trying out for cheerleader one year. Because of him, I didn't try out. I still can't believe that, because it was one of the things I was most proud of and passionate about. Things were bad and about to get worse. The night was coming that would end it all.

We were broken up AGAIN (which was happening on a daily basis), so Peri, Patti, and I decided to hang out at Woodrow Hill with our friends from my J.L Long Junior High days. We had a great time and I ran into my old boyfriend, Howle, and I spent a lot of time talking to him. Before I knew it, I looked around to see Peri and Patti were gone; and I had no way to get home. So Howle offered to drive me home. As we turned on to Van Pelt, my street, I decided to lie down in the seat and asked Howle to tell me if he saw a red Firebird parked in front of my house. He said, "no," but that there was one further down the street. I told him not to stop, so we made the block and parked.

Howle was very concerned because he could sense my anxiety. He asked if I was scared of this guy. I wiped a tear from my eye and said, "No. I just didn't want there to be a scene." I told him I would run between the houses and go in through the garage or the backyard. Howle didn't want to let me go, but I said I would be fine and jumped out of his car. I ran up the alley between Van Pelt and Baumgarten, which was a block over. I got very close to St. Francis, because I was so scared Allen would see me. Then I ran across my street, Van Pelt, until I got to my alley; then ran down to my house. I climbed my wooden fence and jumped into the back yard, trying to keep my German Shepherd Carl from barking and whining. I could tell my dog was very concerned for me. I gave Carl a huge hug, then slipped in through the sliding glass door and sighed deeply. I was safe. I locked the door behind me, went back to my bedroom and turned the light on.

Peri and Patti were there because their car was out front. Peri was asleep in my bed; and Patti was lying down in my childhood room. In true form, my mother was passed out. My mistake was turning the light on. After I did this, I heard a knock at the front door. I went to the door and he was there. Allen pleaded with me to come out and talk to him. I could tell by the way he was talking he had been drinking; and I continued to say, "No!" Somehow he got to me. I can't remember what he said that touched my heart, but he was in tears begging me to just give him a moment. To be honest, I still cared for him so much. I opened the door slightly; and he pounced. He reached in and grabbed me by my arm, pulling me outside and down the front steps with one arm. It happened so fast; behind his back he was holding a tire iron, the thing you use to change a tire. He threw me on the ground and hit me with the metal tool. I began to crawl away and he kicked me over and over. He hit me in the face with the tool. I immediately felt the blood begin to flow. I raised my arms as to shield my face. I couldn't get up because he kept hitting me, but I freed myself and, like a frightened animal, crawled between my house and the neighbor's. I prayed the neighbors would see me out their window, but the house was dark and it appeared no one was awake. I can still feel the wet grass beneath my clothes and taste the blood from my busted lip and cheek. He was out of control and for the first time, I was literally scared for my life. I was crying hysterically and begging him to stop, hoping someone, anyone, would hear the abuse.

At that very moment, Patti came running out of my house. She was wearing her cute denim overalls (which were the fashion at the time) and in her hand she was wielding my Spirit Stick; that my team had won from cheerleading camp during my junior high year. Although genuinely thankful for her attempted rescue, my first thought was, "Couldn't she have found a better weapon?" I mean a spirit stick is a small wooden dowel painted red, white, and blue. I was hoping for the Civil War sword that adorned my fireplace as well as the old musket which was displayed beside it. . .but it was not a time to be critical.

Patti probably saved my life. I am so thankful for her and that spirit stick, because in the future, they would provide me comic relief in this horribly tragic situation. I was on the ground trying to avoid the blows, Allen was standing over me holding the tire iron, and Patti was behind him trying to beat him off with the spirit stick. The only other problem was, she kept missing him! She would raise the spirit stick with both hands, come down and COMPLETELY miss! Every time she missed, she would almost fall down. By this time, I was laughing through the tears and blood. Patti then ran into the house screaming, "Mrs. DeFace, Mrs. DeFace, you have to wake up! Allen is outside beating up Susan!" Something about Patti's action made him stop. He grabbed his tool, ran to his car and left. Patti ran outside to help me to my feet. My mother staggered to the door, still drunk and not sure what was going on. My father was not home. He was at the lake. My mother went back to bed. Patti and I began to tend to my wounds. Somehow, Peri slept through the entire commotion. That was the worst beating; and the last I received from Allen. Not long after that night, Keith, a varsity offensive lineman who was very large, told Allen to never bother me again. He didn't. It was the end to our relationship. Finally I was out of that abusive relationship, but sadly my home life would continue to deteriorate.

My 17th birthday is one that I have always remembered. After arriving home from school, I hurriedly went into the house looking for my mother. With a childlike faith and expectancy, I hoped she would be standing there to greet me, but as I called her name, there was no response. She was most always passed out by this point, but I never knew where I would find her. This day she was on the floor outside of the master bathroom. Walking into the powder room of the bath, I bent down to see if I could hear her breathing and to check her pulse. Knowing she was "okay," I went to kitchen as the phone began to ring. It was my dad calling to say that he wouldn't be coming home again because he was too busy and would be staying at the lake. He had not been home in a long time. He didn't even remember it was my birthday. Sadly, I hung up the phone and went into the den. My spirits were somewhat lifted as I saw birthday presents stacked on the old stereo, I guess mother did it before her drinking began that day. Not sure what to do because I knew she was out for the night, and my dad wouldn't be coming home, I decided to open my presents.

I sat on the blue rug in our den and began to celebrate my 17th birthday by myself. That year I received three gifts: a beautiful light blue sweater, pants to go with it, and a One-Step-Camera, which was a Polaroid and very popular at the time. I was so excited about the camera and opened it quickly so that I could start taking pictures right away. Not being one who has ever read instructions, I loaded it with film and took a picture of our Christmas tree. As the camera spat out my first ever photo, there was nothing on it. Blank. Confused, I took another, then another. This continued to happen until I had used the whole roll of film. Each photo was as blank as the next. I thought the camera didn't work, so I went to try on my new sweater. Excitedly I ran through the powder room, leaping over my mother's passed out body, so I could go into her room and use the full length mirror. The sweater was as pretty as I thought it would be and I smiled at myself in the mirror. When I returned to the den, there were 20 pictures of our Christmas tree!!! I laughed realizing it took a while for the photographs to develop.

The story of the camera was so funny to me; I decided I really should share it with someone. Keith was in my chemistry class and by now I had a huge crush on him. He was a year older than me, was a star football player, and the most popular boy at school. I looked forward to chemistry because it was so fun for me. Keith and I laughed all the time. So the next day in class, I told him my story about the camera. As I got to the part about the 20 pictures of the Christmas tree, I looked up at him expecting to see laughter on his face, but all I saw was sadness and sorrow in his eyes. He touched my arm gently and said,

"You mean you opened your birthday presents all by yourself? Susan, that's the saddest thing I have ever heard."

I can't remember how I responded, but I knew I had let my guard down and mistakenly offered a glimpse into my tragic life. It was a glimpse I didn't want revealed. From then on, I was much more careful. I did not want anyone feeling sorry for me, especially him. I wanted him to see me as cute, funny, and outgoing. Not the way I truly felt: alone, abandoned, unloved, and obviously just so deeply damaged that I didn't matter to anyone. I built another wall that day; and I didn't let my guard down ever again.

CHAPTER 3

The Secret I've Kept Locked Away, No One Can Ever See

Something has been taken from deep inside of me
The secret I've kept locked away no one can ever see
Wounds so deep they never show they never go away
— Linkin Park

Most people from school would probably describe me as a girl who was always smiling with a good sense of humor. I loved school and excelled in academics. My senior year I was nominated head cheerleader and that brought a lot of happiness to me, but it also made me more adamant to keep the secret of my miserable home life. Another wall built. Toward the end of my senior year, my mother's alcoholism was completely out of control. I didn't know how to deal with it on any level. I spent a lot of my time driving around or going to movies alone so I would not have to be in the home with her. My favorite movie was Ice Castles. I went to see it multiple times by myself. It was a story of a young ice skater whose mother had died.

She lived with a father who was emotionally remote. I related to that young girl so well, maybe that is why I went to see it so many times.

Skyline Head Cheerleader: 1978-79

On the special day of my high school's "red and blue" game (the passing of the torch to the next group of cheerleaders, officially marking the end of my school days) my mother almost burned down our house. My closest friend, Peri, had stopped by my home to pick up something for me and the house was on fire. She ran in and found my mother naked in the front room. She managed to put a robe on her, grabbed a few things, and went to a neighbor's house to call the fire department and my father. After making the calls, she discovered my mother was no longer with her. My mother had gone back into our burning house. As Peri went in to get her, my mom told Peri she wanted to die. She had given up.

After the commotion had died down, I went home. My dad had already come and gone. He had returned to the lake and it was just me and my mother. I remember I was still in my cheerleading uniform from the earlier ceremony; it would be my last time to ever wear it. This signified the end to so many things; my childhood, my school days, cheerleading, and as you can imagine, so much more. It was also very close to the end of my mother's life, although I didn't realize that at the time. I guess her words to Peri were true, she just wanted to die and she had given up. To be honest, I think I gave up that day too, I gave up my burning hope that she would quit drinking and that my dad would come home. I think I knew the situation was hopeless; and I didn't know how much longer any of us could go on. I didn't know if I could take much more. Humiliated and embarrassed by what had happened are the only words I have to describe what I felt. Thank God it was Peri who found her, that was bad enough, but not as bad as if it had been someone else. Peri was my best friend. I had tried so hard to keep my mother's alcoholism a secret. Now the neighbors knew. They not only knew, but they saw how truly bad it was. I was overwhelmed with shame. I thought her behavior reflected what type of person I was. That was a heavy burden for an 18 year old girl to bear.

I stood up and walked to her doorway and watched her. Literally, she was out of her mind. The mattress to her bed had been destroyed by the fire, leaving only the frame and headboard. I guess she didn't realize that because she had sheets and was trying to make the bed as if there was a mattress. She would throw the sheet over the frame, trip over it, fall, then get up and try again. I stood there watching nervously, chewing on the tip of my thumb. At times I would laugh nervously because it was just so disturbing and I didn't know what to do. She was not even aware I was there. I felt invisible and so alone. For the first time, bitterness and contempt started to rise within me and I hated her. I was so tired of everything: taking care of her, pretending I was okay, pretending my parents were okay, and this list could go on. After she had fallen into the frame again, I was scared she was going to really hurt herself. I went to help her to her feet and guided her to my old bedroom. I put my mom in my old bed. Covering her with a blanket, I walked towards the door and turned off the light. As I shut the door, I took one last look at her. I went to my room to get ready for whatever plans I had that night. Later, as I was leaving, I walked into the room to check on her, just to make sure she was breathing and alive. My "normal" each day, for as long as I can remember, before I left and when I got home, the first thing I did was make sure she was alive.

After the fire and the spectacle of what happened in my life, I was feeling pretty hopeless. All I knew to do was move forward the best I could. It wasn't long after the fire episode that my mother went through the worse delirium tremens that I had ever seen. It was night and she was in my old bedroom, thrashing about in the bed and screaming that spiders were attacking her. I tried to calm her down, but knew I needed to get her to the hospital. I had learned from experience how serious this was, that she could die and needed medical attention. My problem was getting my mother to the car by myself. She was naked, having hallucinations, and shaking violently. The thought of calling for help never occurred to me, even though, at this point, the neighbors knew something was wrong and I had nothing to hide. The lingering sense of shame and embarrassment I felt were crushing. I left her room, trying to think of what to do and how to do it, when she got up and started running. The hallucinations she was having were terrifying to her and me. She went out the front door and I frantically ran after her. After catching her, and a lot of struggle, I got a robe on her, and somehow got her in my car. We drove to Doctor's Hospital where she detoxed. I can't remember how long my mom was there, but it was at least a few days because I remember having to return to visit her. She was still very delirious, but was slowly coming out of the fog. The memory of sitting on the end of her bed at Doctor's Hospital is still very vivid. This would be the most coherent I would see her before her death. Maybe that is why I remember it. I don't recall talking. I just remember being with her.

After she got home from the hospital, the drinking began again. I had someone ask me at that time where she got the alcohol since she was always so drunk. I didn't know the answer.

After detoxing at the hospital, within a day or two, she was back to being passed out every day. The senior prom was my next special event to happen. It was in May. On prom night, my date came to pick me up. My mother was passed out in the den and I think my father was at the lake. There was no one to take my picture or see me off. When my date arrived, I wanted to get out of the house as quickly as possible because I didn't want him to see her. I was so afraid she would wake up and do something awful. He asked me about taking pictures. I just shrugged. I didn't knowing what to do or say, I just wanted to get out of there.

Me, in my prom dress taken a few days before the dance.

Next, would be graduation. Our school had hundreds of graduates and the ceremony seemed to go on forever. It was hot in the Dallas Convention Center. The main thing I remember is all my friends meeting their parents and families, getting hugs and congratulations. I, once again, was alone. As I walked through the crowds, I looked anxiously for my father, hoping and praying he had made it there for me. I was so proud I had graduated with honors and I thought he would be proud too. I knew my mother wouldn't be there because she was already passed out when I left the house earlier. I surely thought my dad would be there for me. He wasn't. . . I was heartbroken and felt numb. No one had come to support me. As I looked around, I was certain everyone knew that no one had come for me. The hurt and pain were incomprehensible, but by this point, I was angry too. I think on some level, I thought that if I achieved enough and was popular enough my parents would change and pay attention to me. Little did I know, I did not have that power. No matter how amazingly I performed, they were not going to change until they dealt with their own pain. Sadly, this never happened.

That night I went to graduation parties and got very drunk. The alcohol dismissed my self-control and I remember crying uncontrollably. It was a horrible feeling believing that I didn't matter to anyone. The next day was a Sunday and I went to the lake with my boyfriend to go water skiing. We had a lot of fun and I was able to forget the pain from the day before. I arrived home fairly late that night and was exhausted, so I went straight to my room. After changing clothes, my mother staggered into my bedroom door. I hated her and was just so tired of dealing with her. So much had happened in the last few weeks and I think I blamed her for everything: for my dad leaving, for no one helping make my prom magical, and no one coming to see and be proud of me for graduating with honors. She was very, very drunk and had to grab the door frame to steady herself. She just looked at me not saying one word. Looking at her, I was filled with contempt and I told her "get the ^%&$ out of my room. I hate you and I wish you were dead."

Those words would be the last I ever said to her. The look of hurt and sadness on her face is embedded in my memory. She backed out of my room and I slammed the door shut and went to sleep. The next day, which was Memorial Day, I slept very late, until almost noon. My friend Cheri and I were heading to Lake Ray Hubbard to lie out in the sun. We had been working hard on our tans as we were getting ready for our graduation trip to Hawaii. When I woke up, I walked down the hall to the kitchen to get something to drink and eat. As I passed my childhood room where my mom now slept because of the fire, I thought my mother was sleeping in. I paused because I didn't hear her. Her breathing was always labored and could be heard easily. I couldn't hear a thing. It was silent. Walking into my childhood room was like walking into a time warp because it had remained unchanged from when I was a little girl .The stuffed animals were still arranged in one corner, my baby dolls were in their carriages, my favorite Little Kittle House was still set up, my Barbie dolls were in place, and the room was decorated with white princess furniture that every girl I knew seemed to have. I called out, "Momma." She didn't respond. Her back was to me, so I walked closer and said, "Momma" again, but still no response. I bent over to shake her awake and when I touched her, her skin was so very cold and clammy. As I turned her over, she felt rigid. Her face was surprisingly distorted; and her hands were swollen to the point that I couldn't see her rings. I turned and left the room as fast as I could. Deep down I knew she was dead. Admitting it was something I didn't want to face. I was alone in the house, with her, and horrified. I remembered what I had said the night before. I hated myself for saying those words to her; and I honestly thought I had killed her.

I went into the kitchen and called my dad at the lake. I told him something was wrong and I couldn't wake mother up. He argued with me saying she was just passed out. At that point, I began to beg him to come home reiterating that something was really wrong with momma. He finally agreed to come and I hung up the phone. I called Cheri to tell her something was wrong and I wasn't sure what it was, but that I couldn't go tanning. I went and sat on the floor in the den and turned on the TV. "All My Children," the soap opera, was on. I sat on our blue shag rug in our sunken den staring at the television trying not to think about anything. Cedar Creek Lake, where our lake house was, was about an hour away from our home. My father would be with me then. Not knowing what to do, I just rocked back and forth gently — waiting for my dad to arrive. The next thing I can remember is that a fire truck, ambulance, and possibly a coroner arrived at my house. I am not sure exactly who came but it certainly caused a commotion in the neighborhood. As had happened a few weeks earlier, when she started the fire, the neighbors were outside on their front lawns concerned and curious about what was happening. Luckily a friend of mine gathered me up and we went to Pizza Getti to get something to eat. That restaurant was a comforting place for me.

The guilt I felt when I said those last words to my mom was staggering. In my teenage mind, I knew I couldn't share this with anyone, ever. I knew they would think I was horrible and that I killed her. And I really thought my words might have killed her. I pushed it down. I pushed it down deep. I pretended none of that happened. Logically, I knew it had.

I remember various people trying to comfort me, but I would not let my guard down. I never even cried in front of one person. It was extremely hard, but I was determined not to show any emotion. At times I could be so stoic.

At one point, I slipped away by myself and went to the funeral home. A lady who worked there asked me if I wanted to see my mom. I said, "Yes." Thankfully she left me alone and as I looked at my mother in the casket, I totally fell apart and lost complete control. I remember just throwing myself at the casket, hitting it with my arms and pleading forgiveness. I hit the casket so hard I caused bruising on my arms.

The scene must have been very disturbing because the lady came running into the room where the casket was and tried to stop me. Concerned, she started hugging me, telling me it was going to be okay. She started crying. I think because she was not sure how to help me. Embarrassed, I regained my composure. I knew it was never going to be okay because I believed I had killed my mom. I was never going to have a chance to apologize for saying those words to her. I hated myself as I walked to my car to return home.

After the funeral, things returned to "normal." My dad went back to the lake house and I stayed in the house on Van Pelt by myself. This proved to be one of the darkest times in my life. Having no skills to cope with day to day life, or the tools to even begin the grieving process, I just shut the door to the room where she died and never went in there. I felt a paralyzing fear all the time. I also closed the doors to the room where my brother David died. This simple act made me think I could shut out all the darkness; and it would not consume me.

That summer I had the most disturbing recurring nightmares. This evil dream came every night. In the nightmare I would be in the house and then my mother and brother would appear in clown makeup. They were riding tricycles, chasing and taunting me. They would be screaming what a horrible excuse of a person I was and why hadn't I been a better daughter to my mother. They would accuse me of killing her.

I always woke up in a cold sweat, crying uncontrollably. Remember, I was all alone in that house where they both died such tragic deaths. I felt so isolated from the world and everyone in it. It was such a horrific experience for me. I'm disturbed even now as I write about it.

At the end of the summer, my father moved back from the lake house, but he did not move in with me. He moved in with his girlfriend and her two daughters. They lived two streets over and were people I had known growing up. There was not enough room for me to live there, so again, I stayed in the house on Van Pelt by myself. I felt discarded. Like no one wanted me. That gruesome nightmare persisted. My feeling of isolation swelled. Still thinking I had caused my mother's death, I didn't share the nightmare with anyone. I tried to pretend I was well, so no one would find out how awful I really was. My sister was living very far away. My dad had a new family and I didn't feel welcome. There was no one to turn to, the loneliness was crippling. To be honest, I am amazed that I could function.

That fall and the next spring, I went to Eastfield Jr. College and functioned to some extent, pretending to be okay. It still astonishes me that I went to class and took a full schedule. There was some kind of strength and drive in me that kept me moving forward. God must have planted this in me. I don't know and I don't care, but to this day I am so thankful to HIM for watching over me.

48 | From Pom Poms to Prison

Seemingly on top of the world, no one knew my pain.

Smiling was the façade I used to hide my pain.

CHAPTER 4

You Think You Have A Memory, But It Has You

Your memory is a monster; you forget—it doesn't. It simply files things away. It keeps things for you, or hides things from you—and summons them to your recall with will of its own. You think you have a memory; but it has you!
— John Irving, A Prayer for Owen Meany

During the spring of my first year at Eastfield, I made a trip to Fayetteville, Arkansas. I went to visit a boy that I had known from vacationing there in the past. He attended the University of Arkansas and was in a fraternity. We had met when I was in ninth grade at the Shangri-La resort on Lake Ouachita. Ironically, our families, who didn't know each other at all, reserved cabins on the lake at the same time each summer. Seeing him every summer was a lot of fun and something I looked forward to. We both loved to water ski and play tennis. He was the best water skier I had ever seen and was the one who taught me to ski barefoot. . sort of. I could never fully master it, although I could barefoot for a little bit. I will always remember how patient he was with me as I tried to learn. We would spend our days on the lake skiing and swimming. We liked each other a lot, but he lived in Arkansas and I lived in Dallas. It would have been a long distant relationship and surely difficult.

Although we did phone each other and write letters during the school year, the relationship wasn't anything more than a summer romance. During the spring of 1980, he asked me to come to a big fraternity party at his college in Fayetteville. I was excited to go because it had been such an emotionally tough year for me. I thought just getting away would make things better, plus I did really like him and enjoyed his company. Besides, he had come to Dallas to visit me the previous summer, after my mom died. I was somewhat nervous about going, I had not seen him in a year and I had put on some weight. The previous summer, I had been the thinnest I had ever been, preparing to look great for my trip to Hawaii. Unfortunately, as the year progressed, I slowly put on weight as I had used food to comfort the extreme pain I felt inside. Frankly, I was a mess. After arriving in Fayetteville, I got a hotel room and he picked me up to go to the first of many planned parties for the weekend. What should have been a fun-filled weekend for me started turning traumatic. He didn't do anything wrong, it was just me. As I said, I was a mess. The emotional damage from my mother's death and living alone in that house were taking a toll. Maybe it was being in an unfamiliar city with people I didn't know. The loneliness was magnified in the situation.

I woke up on Saturday morning in the hotel room by myself and felt desperate. Out of the blue, I decided to call my sister. (I'm sure I had to call collect because there were not cell phones at the time.) I just started talking to her in a rambling fashion. She asked me if I was okay, I nodded to no one and said "yes," but my voice started trembling. Then I lost all control and started crying, telling her I didn't know what was wrong, that I felt totally hopeless in the moment. This was so out of character for me because I usually just held everything in. I fell apart that day. My sweet sister jumped into action and wired money to me. Within an hour, I was in a cab on the way to the airport and on a plane to Amarillo. This is where I would stay for the summer and through the fall semester. I felt horrible for leaving so suddenly, but as I walked off that plane into my sister's arms, I felt like I had finally arrived "home," a home that genuinely felt like home.

Kathey rescued me that day; and I felt unconditional love for the first time in my life. I loved being with her. This was a time of happiness for me because I was living with a family: a family that functioned like a family. We sat down and ate dinner, went to church, and did things together. It was very strange to me. Warmly, it was so wonderful to have someone to talk to, someone who cared where I was and if I came home, and truly to be in a relationship with others. Looking back, I realize that Kathey's home was the first place I saw Jesus and unconditional love, even though I didn't recognize it at the time. I ended up staying in the Amarillo area and went to college at West Texas State University, where I received a degree in education. I believe my college experience was much like others. There was quite a bit of partying, but the people I ran around with did not do drugs. I did drink a lot at times. When I did, my guard would drop and an extreme sadness would descend upon me, causing me to sob deeply about the death of my mom.

My Pa Pa who killed himself just like David.

In the fall of 1981, I lost my grandfather to suicide. A pattern was beginning to form. Suicide seemed to run in our family. I was living in an apartment in Amarillo and commuting to school at West Texas State University, in Canyon Texas, which was about 20 miles away. One morning, I woke up and immediately remembered my dream from that night before which was unnerving. I dreamed that my Pa Pa and my brother David were sitting on a couch, hugging, and talking. That was all I remembered. I never dreamt of my Pa Pa and the last dreams I had of David were the recurring nightmare I had after mother died that frightened me so badly. So I was relieved and comforted that I had dreamed something pleasant and not ghastly. As I was getting ready to drive to class, I received a phone call from my sister saying my Pa Pa had died, but she wasn't sure of the details. We flew to Dallas for the services, but my father would never tell us how Pa Pa died. My dad was evasive that way — so emotionally remote. I didn't feel I could approach him and ask what had or how it had happened. It was later that I learned that he took a gun, put it to his temple, and took his own life, just like David. After learning how my Pa Pa died, I remembered my dream and thought it was ironic that I dreamed of them together, on the very night he died. Honestly, it upset me more than I can explain.

It was during college that I met my husband. One night, a friend and I were out at a country-western bar called *The Wrangler* and two young men asked us to dance. They ended up sitting at the table with us; and we had a lot of fun. The boy who showed interest in me was named Warner. Later he asked me if I wanted to go to a fraternity party with him the next night. He seemed very nice, and since we were having such fun, I said "yes." I said I would meet him the next night at the party, and I did. We began to date exclusively after that. He was a senior at West Texas State and would be graduating in the summer of 1982.

Meeting Warner opened a door into my college experience that I had not experienced yet. I was living in Amarillo in an apartment, going to school, and didn't really have too many friends. He encouraged me to move to the dorm so I could meet people and engage. I took that advice and it was a good move, as I made more friends. After moving to Canyon, I spent most of my time with Warner and his group of friends. This was a lot of fun for me. I finally felt like I belonged to a group again. It is a basic need we have to feel as if we belong; and that was missing from my life. A lot of our time was spent partying, but this was a good group of kids. Most of this group smoked marijuana and they did experiment with other drugs, but graduating from college was their goal and they all achieved it. This would be my first introduction to any drugs other than marijuana, so in hindsight, I can see where this opened the door slightly for me to think a little drug use was okay, although I never participated. As I have stated before, I never smoked pot, but only because I didn't like it, not for any moral reasons. In my mind, marijuana was okay, but hard drugs were not. So when they dabbled in that, I just said "no."

Proudly in 1985 I received my Bachelor of Science degree from West Texas State University. At first I wasn't going to go to the graduation ceremony because I didn't think it was important but I probably didn't want to set myself up for the same disappointment that I experienced at my high school graduation. My sister insisted and I finally relented. My father didn't make it, he said college graduation wasn't important like high school so he would pass. I wanted to remind him that he didn't attend my high school graduation but I chose as usual where he was concerned to remain silent. Warner, Kathey, and her family came to cheer me on and it was a proud day for me.

CHAPTER 5
It's A Slow Fade

It's a slow fade when you give yourself away
It's a slow fade when black and white have turned to gray
Thoughts invade, choices are made, a price will be paid
When you give yourself away
People never crumble in a day
It's a slow fade; it's a slow fade
- Casting Crowns

Not long after college, I got married, started my family and my career as a public school special education teacher. Teaching was wonderful for me. I excelled with students who were considered challenging. I truly believe God created me to work with students who have disabilities because he gave me a compassionate and merciful nature. I have three children who have been such a blessing to me: Hailey born in 1988, Alexis born in 1992, and Sammy who was born in 1993. Those first years of teaching were a calm time in my life. It was like the pain was dormant. It was buried so deep within me, I thought it was gone. During this time, I continued to drink a lot, but didn't think I had a problem because I wasn't drinking perfume or going through DTs when I didn't drink. Despite being a wife, parent, and professional educator, I also experimented with drugs more during this time.

My kids in the tub

As I said before, I didn't do drugs in high school or college, I didn't even use marijuana. I did drink, but I justified my drinking because I wasn't passed out all the time and I didn't reek of perfume and rubbing alcohol. The drug use started innocently enough, after seeing a doctor for weight loss pills. The feeling I had on those pills was something I really liked so I often increased my dosage. Then I tried Cocaine and wasn't too crazy about it, but I liked the feeling of speeding. Then came Meth; and it was something I loved: you felt on top of the world and invincible: you could get a lot done, and you could drink a lot of alcohol and not get drunk. Initially, Meth was not something I did all that often; it was just something I really enjoyed and did every now and then.

In 1996 we decided to move back to the Dallas area so my husband could find a better job. We had been married 10 years; and Hailey was 7, Alexis 4, and Sammy 3. This was a good move for us and we settled down in Rockwall. I was so blessed to be hired as the Special Education Coordinator for Campbell ISD and I loved that job. It was a smaller district and I was able to bring in some innovative ideas for the special education department. My husband got a great job in sales at Glazer and my kids went to school with me. This was one of the happiest times of my life; and we were doing well. It seemed almost too good to be true. It was, because my world was about to come crashing down once again.

In 1998, my sister Kathey, who was my rock and anchor, was diagnosed with cancer. Not long after the diagnosis, we knew she wasn't going to make it much longer. The idea of losing her was too much for me. I had spent a lifetime tucking grief away, pretending it didn't exist, but I couldn't do that anymore. I just didn't have it in me. Fear, extreme pain, and hopelessness set in. Honestly, when I thought of her being gone forever, I had physical pain in my heart. There was no support system in place, no relationship with God, just me, by myself, trying to cope. The only thing that made me feel better was Meth. And as I did Meth, the fear, pain, and hopelessness slipped away. So I started doing Meth regularly to numb the pain I was feeling.

Kathey died on Memorial Day 1999 at the age of 49. It was ironic because my mother died on Memorial Day 1979 at the age of 49 also. Her funeral was the following Thursday in the Panhandle. My life was already falling apart because of my drug use, but I was still functioning to some extent. As I traveled with my father to Amarillo to bury my sister, the pain I felt was incomprehensible. There was literally physical pain in my heart when I thought of her being gone forever. To this day, I have never experienced pain like that again, even with the recent death of my father. At the time I only knew to numb the pain; and I did that more and more frequently with Meth.

Arriving home from the funeral, I went to my dad's house where I had left my car. As I was about to leave, he was standing in the doorway of the garage, a broken man, completely devastated by the loss of his oldest child, as he had never recovered from the suicide of my brother. He looked at me and said, "You are okay, Susan, aren't you? Some people are worried about you, but YOU ARE OKAY?" and he was nodding his head trying to make it true. I will never forget standing there looking at him in his complete brokenness and pausing for what seemed like an eternity. I was not okay on any level, but he wanted me to be so bad; and I didn't want to disappoint him. Plus, I could not verbalize the truth. The fear of the truth paralyzed me and thoughts bombarded my mind. I thought that if I was honest, I would lose my job, my kids, and my life would be ruined. So I looked him in the eye, smiled sadly, and said, "I am fine Daddy," then turned around and went home. I bought the lie that day, kept my horrible secret and continued to use drugs.

Eventually all that I feared happened but on a much larger scale: I lost my job and my career, CPS got my kids, and my life fell apart.

That was the first fork in my road, where, looking back, I see that if I could have just said "I need help, please help me," it might have been different. Please don't get me wrong, I am not playing the "what if" game, because that is not healthy. When we speak the truth, God will set us free and it removes the heavy burden we are carrying. But for me, I chose the lie and the destruction in my life started to gather speed. I was about to lose any control I had.

My life spiraled into a Meth addiction that was dark and evil. This drug is straight from Satan and it completely destroys peoples' lives. Once I was hooked, it didn't numb the pain anymore, it just led me on a path of self-destruction. I was missing so much work, and my kids were missing so much school, that I was asked to leave Campbell ISD, where just a few years before I was considered one of their top employees. They let me resign and said they would give me a good recommendation, so I was able to get hired at nearby Garland ISD. At Lakeview Centennial High School, I was employed as a Life Skills Teacher.

My classes of students at Lakeview were a special group of kids and I loved them so much, but I was a mess. The drug had taken over my life and was affecting the lives of my children, because both Warner and I were hopeless addicts using daily. Our life was spiraling out of control at a very fast rate, changing our personalities, our priorities, our morals and values. Warner, my husband, was arrested on a possession charge in Dallas and was sentenced to County Jail for one month. He qualified for a work release program (although I don't know how because he was not working), so he was released during the day and had to return at night. I had just picked him up from Decker (the work release detention facility), when we were fighting horribly. Addiction had ruined our relationship. He was mad because I had done a lot of our drugs the night before and the fight had turned physical. As we passed the Lawnview exit, I decided to get out of the car because I was scared he would really hurt me. I just had to get out. As I opened the door, my husband slowed down and began to pull over screaming at me to stop, not sure of what I was going to do. When he slowed down enough to where I could get out, I jumped out of the car and started running. Tears were streaming down my face. I felt so very lost and alone. I ran into Grove Hill Cemetery and decided to look for my mother and brother's site. I didn't have a clue where they were buried, but I needed to find them desperately. I needed my momma. I ran up and down rows looking for the DeFace name. I found them, which was amazing because Grove Hill is huge! After finding the markers with their names, I just threw myself down on my mother's site crying my heart out.

I was crying for the mother I missed so badly and never really knew in life, crying for the girl I had been with hopes and dreams, for the little girl who had been so neglected, and for the sad addicted woman I had become. I knew my life was out of control, but I didn't have the tools or the strength to make the changes I needed to turn it around. I will never forget that moment of sheer desperation and total helplessness. I know God led me to my mother, giving me one more chance to reach out, but I couldn't. Maybe my selfish pride prevented me from admitting what I had become. I just stood up wearily, brushing the grass off my clothes. I looked back and saw my husband parked, watching me, and crying too. As I walked to the car, he said that was the saddest thing he had ever seen: me running through the cemetery looking for my dead mother. Not knowing how to respond, I just got into the car and leaned back, exhausted from the experience. Sadly, we drove to our home to do some more drugs.

I believe God has his hand on our lives, protecting us when we don't deserve it. But if we continue in disobedience, he sometimes has to withdraw his protection so we can fall. And sometimes HE has to throw a brick in our window to get our attention.

During the fall and winter of 2000, we were "friends" with some people who were drug dealers and users who happened to cook Meth. We would help them get the ingredients to make the drug and then they would give us a portion. Finding the ingredients could be quite a challenge.

When we first met Tanner and his girlfriend, Letta, it seemed everything was going great for them. They had a lot of money, cars, apartments in town and out of town, and a lot of drugs. To be honest, I thought they were nice people but in reality, they were just drug addicts like me. The fall of 2000 was hard on them, getting busted twice for manufacturing, but making bail both times. I was secretly pulling for them, hoping the lifestyle they were living could work out, but as I saw them falling apart, I refused to see the truth of the situation: their life was a mirror image of mine. I was just a few months, and a few charges, behind them. In hindsight, this was an incredible gift from God. He allowed me to witness their lives as they slowly self-destructed, hoping I would learn from it. At times, I am so in awe of HIS grace and mercy for me, even when I was so disrespectful to HIM.

Despite their run-ins with the law, I was hoping Tanner and Letta could get it together. When they got busted the third time for manufacturing, I helped them when they got out of jail. I rented them a car and loaned them some money. Their days of money, cars, and even drugs, were gone. They had lost everything. Each time they got busted, police confiscated a car, as well as all their cash.

After borrowing money from me, they disappeared. I was desperate to find them and called all the time. The rental car they had was in my name and they owed me cash. I wanted the car and my money or, at the very least, some Meth! Finally, one day, I called Tanner's phone and he answered. I yelled at him and he said he finally had something he could give me. Angry, and intent on being repaid, I drove to meet him at a Motel 6 on Highway 80 in Mesquite.

Before I left my house, Tanner called and asked me to bring a pan — one that would withstand heat — for cooking Meth. Pulling into the parking space at the motel, I paused and thought for a moment. I had an empty 12 pack of cokes in my car and for some reason; I decided to put the Pyrex pan in the 12 pack container. This was not typical behavior for me, as I wasn't scared of being watched by the police. In my opinion, the police needed to be looking for the real criminals! (Manufacturing and using a little Meth was not that bad. I was in such denial!) So I got out of my car, still very angry at Tanner, and knocked on the door. When he answered, my anger melted away. He was a wreck! He had no money, no food, no cigarettes and he was not having any success at making the Meth.

My heart broke for him. I told him to let me run to the store and get him some food and cigarettes. Driving over to the Race Track on Buckner Blvd, I just felt bad for him; he had lost everything. I bought the items from the store and drove back to the motel. Tanner and I started talking as he ate his sandwiches; the Meth he was attempting to make was cooking in the bathroom. He was talking about how he hoped he was successful this time, so he could make some money because he had all these charges against him. At that time, there was a loud knock on the door. . .banging to be exact. We paused and at that moment, the door was broken down and DEA agents flooded the room. They were wearing protective gear and had machine guns. I am not a gun expert, but they looked like high-powered weapons to me. It was like a scene from a movie. They told us to lie on the ground on our stomachs and not move. I guess I wasn't moving fast enough because a man came and threw me to the ground, with a gun to my head. I don't think I have ever been that frightened. They searched the room and took us outside to separate us.

This was the last straw for Tanner. It was his fourth manufacturing charge and although there was no Meth manufactured yet, it was obvious what he was doing. Then they questioned me. The lead officer asked me what I was doing there. He asked about the 12 pack of cokes I had brought in and going to the Race Track. (They knew everything I bought down to the last detail, so I know they followed me.) He asked if I knew what Tanner was doing. I told him that I had come to the motel to get money that Tanner owed me; and that, when I arrived, I felt bad for him, so I went and bought him some things. (I didn't tell him I brought him a pan to cook Meth in; the coke package saved me on that.) The officer stopped talking to me, went over to talk with Tanner, then returned. He asked if he could search my car and I nodded. The search came up clean and then they let me go. I could not believe it; they let me go!!!!

Tanner was then loaded into the DEA agent's car and transported to the Federal Prison in Seagoville, Texas, where he ended up serving a very long sentence. Tanner confirmed that I had nothing to do with his manufacturing. He could have told them I brought him a pan, but he chose to protect me.

This was the first brick God ever threw in my window to get my attention. I had two choices that day: to change the way I was living my life because I saw where the lifestyle would lead or continue in my addiction. But as I drove away that day, my only thought was, "Where am I going to get my Meth now?"

I didn't recognize or appreciate the blessing I had received. I just thought I would always be lucky. But my luck had actually run out that day. The string of events that followed that very close call led to my own arrest on April 19th, 2001.

It is not healthy to play the "if only" game in your head. But for the sake of my story, it shows that I could have easily avoided a lot of trouble and legal charges if I would have taken a different path after that experience. My hopes are for those reading my story to see the different forks in the road and try to choose the right way - God's way - as it is never too late. It is so much easier to learn from other's mistakes!

CHAPTER 6
The Darkest Hour Comes Before The Dawn

What just happened to him, laying down like that, was the worst thing he could imagine. And you know what? He found out it was okay. The darkest hour comes before the dawn. That was Pilgrims darkest hour and he survived it.
— *The Horse Whisperer*

THERE ARE MOMENTS THAT MARK YOUR LIFE, MOMENTS WHEN YOU REALIZE NOTHING WILL EVER BE THE SAME AND TIME IS DIVIDED INTO TWO PARTS, "BEFORE THIS MOMENT" AND "AFTER THIS MOMENT." I am not sure where I saw this written but it resonated with my heart. I have had many of these moments in my life: the deaths of my brother, mother, sister, and dad are most prevalent but what happened April 19, 2001, was a transcending moment that marked my life forever.

I was still teaching a Life Skills Class at Lakeview Centennial High School in Garland, TX. I got up (although to be honest I don't think I had gone to sleep because of the drug use) and got ready to leave for work. Earlier in the week, I had learned CPS talked to all three of my children at school. They were scared; and I was terrified. I had called CPS the day of the visit; and had planned on going to their office to speak to them, but the best laid plans fall by the wayside when you are doing drugs, so I never made it. As I looked in the mirror before I left that day, I didn't even recognize the girl looking back at me. I was so very tired and worn out. Being a drug addict is exhausting. It is an endless cycle that never stops. You are never satisfied!!! You think, "Okay, if I can just get some more drugs, then I will be okay," but when you do, you are then worried about running out and where you will get more. It was never-ending and just grueling on my mind, body, and soul. As I walked out the door and got in my car, I sighed wearily and drove to school. Little did I know as I drove away that day, I would never return to that home again; I never even set foot inside of it.

Meth is a horrible, horrible drug and it makes you distracted. You start things you never finish; you can focus on something so insignificant for hours and never get anything accomplished. (I completely destroyed a computer trying to fix it, not to mention the transmission I worked on, totally disabling a car forever but we won't go into that). So that morning, as usual, I drove to school in a rush. It was a Thursday and on Thursdays we took our students out to eat at different restaurants. In our Life Skills class, we spent a lot of time on basic living skills: eating out, shopping at the grocery store, counting money, and going to work. The students had various jobs within the community to teach employment skills. Thursdays were a favorite for everyone. That particular day we went to Spring Creek BBQ off of 190 and 78 for lunch. (The significance of eating there and later getting a job at Dickey's BBQ right up the road would be meaningful to me. I would come full circle then, and to be honest, I have come full circle so often I feel as if I am running around in circles most the time.)

After arriving at school, we started our day and prepared for our field trip. Field Trips were a lot of fun but also a lot of work. Many of the students were in wheelchairs and a few wore diapers so we had to make sure everyone was changed and ready to go. There were also students with specific medical needs to be addressed before we left. Finally, with everyone ready and excited, we loaded the bus and were on our way. We went to the grocery store first to buy a few items then to the restaurant. After eating, we loaded back into the bus and returned to the school. As we pulled into the parking lot, I noticed my car was still there, which surprised me because my husband was supposed to come get it. At this point, we were down to one car that my father had given me. (The other car had been totaled and I had let our insurance lapse.) As I walked into my classroom, I decided to call my husband to see why he had not come to get the car. (At this point we were also down to one phone, a pre-paid cell.) The phone rang a few times and then a man whose voice I didn't recognize answered. I asked for Warner and he said Warner wasn't available.

"Who is this?" I asked.

It was the Rockwall County Sheriff's department. My husband and two other people had been arrested for manufacturing Meth at my home. And they really wanted to talk to me. I didn't know what to do, so I just hung up the phone. Looking around and feeling panicked, I knew I needed to get out of that school. I wanted to figure out what was going on, but I needed to leave that school because I was scared they were on their way to arrest me; and I had drugs in my car.

My assistant walked into the room and I told her I had an emergency and needed to leave. As I walked out of my classroom and said goodbye to my students, I had no idea if I would ever see any of them again. As was the case with my home, I never stepped back inside that school again. Or any school for that matter. That was my very last day as a teacher.

I hurried to the parking lot to get in my car. Meth tends to make people very paranoid and as I was walking, I looked around skittishly, scared there were policemen watching and waiting to arrest me. But I got into my car and drove away. At this point, I really wasn't sure what was going on. All I knew is that I had talked to someone who said he was with the Rockwall Sheriff's Department and my husband did not come get the car nor did he have our phone.

It was about 2:00 in the afternoon, so I knew it wouldn't be long until my kids got out of school. I was so frightened and just didn't know what to do. I needed to confirm where my husband was, so I stopped to use a pay phone. I called the Rockwall County Jail and asked if a Warner Washington was being held. They said "yes" and started listing off the charges. The list was long, and manufacturing Meth was one of the charges, so I knew what I had been told was true. Shaking, I hung up the phone and returned to the car. Driving around aimlessly, I decided to go to Rockwall and pick up my kids from school. My thought was, "I wasn't at the house, so how could I be charged?" Driving into the city limits and exiting Ridge Road, toward the school, was terrifying but I continued on my way.

As I approached the intersection where 205 and Ridge Road/740 split, I pulled into the parking lot of the 7-Eleven and stopped. There was a battle waging within me: I needed to get rid of the drugs I had, but the drug addict within me was stronger than anything else (the mother, wife, teacher, etc.) and was in complete control. I couldn't . .no, wouldn't. . throw the drugs away, but I didn't want them on me when I went to get the kids, so I hid them in the phone booth, planning to retrieve them later. I pulled away and started for the school, but I was scared. .terrified. . I was about to be arrested, so I did what any good drug addict would do: I decided to go back and get my drugs, do the drugs, and then decide what to do. (This is so hard to admit. . that I was more worried about my drugs than anything else, but that is how strong and debilitating addiction can be.)

Driving back to 7-Eleven, I got my stuff and left Rockwall. I was running out of time because I knew my kids would be getting out of school and there was going to be no one to get them. I drove up 66 and stopped at the Eckerd's Drugstore on 66 and Rowlett Road to use the phone again. I knew CPS was investigating us because the kids had been interviewed at school. I had been in contact with CPS, but didn't keep my appointment, so I decided to call the investigator. When the investigator got on the phone, she informed me that CPS had already been to the school and my children were in their custody. When CPS stopped by our home earlier that day for a home visit, my husband was being arrested. My children were currently in the custody of Child Protective Services. I was then informed that I needed to turn myself in because I, too, had a warrant for my arrest.

Shaking, I put the phone back on the hook and left the store, not knowing what to do. My kids were gone, my husband locked up, and I had no money and nowhere to go, so I just got in my car, finished what drugs I had, and drove around trying to come up with a plan.

As I spiraled into my drug addiction, all my friendships changed. There was a group of girls (Peri, Leah, Melanie, Cheri) that I had been friends with since kindergarten, and we had always remained in touch. But as my addiction worsened, I distanced myself from these girls because they weren't doing what I was doing. My circle of so-called friends at the time were all drug addicts like myself. Friendships based on drugs do not run very deep. Don't get me wrong, I am not judging anyone; we were just a lost group of people addicted to drugs. I don't know any of their stories, but I am sure they are filled with pain and dysfunction, like mine. Addiction is so very deceptive and cunning. I would do a mental checklist to see how I was doing compared to my new friends; I always came out on top. I had a job. I graduated from college, as well as high school. I had a car, etc. So in my mind, I didn't have a bad problem because I wasn't like them. Wow, how insane my thinking was back then; it still amazes me how off I was.

I owned some land on old South Central Expressway that I inherited from my grand-daddy which I rented to someone who used it for an Auto Salvage Yard. I rented another building to a man who worked on cars. I needed money now, and rent wasn't due until the first of May, but I thought I might be able to get the rent early, so I decided to make a call. Frank, who ran the auto salvage yard, told me I could come out the next day and he would pay me. Breathing a sigh of relief, all I needed to worry about was that night and where I was going to stay. I was in Rowlett so I decided to stop by Cheri's for a little bit. To be honest, I don't know what I said was going on, but I just stayed there and made a few calls. I then went by Melanie's but she was not home so I just started driving again. I ended up driving around all night long. I have never been homeless, so I can't even possibly understand that, but the feeling I had that night was horrible. There was just nowhere to go. The only family member left at the time was my dad and I was too scared to call him. So I just wandered aimlessly, driven by fear and feeling so very alone in the world. (That is another lie I deal with on a regular basis, especially since the death of my Dad, that I am all alone in this world.) Very early on Friday morning, I stopped by Melanie's again and she was a life saver. I wasn't honest about what all was going on because I was a drug addict and drug addicts lie, but I was honest that I needed help with a place to stay. She gave me some money and I got a motel room and finally laid down to rest. I was emotionally, mentally, and physically exhausted.

After I slept for a little bit (at the Budget Suites off Jupiter and Kingsley in Garland) I got some food at the Waffle House around the corner. It is amazing how I remember, in detail, what I ordered. I got a Patty Melt with Fries and a Coke. To this day, that is my favorite thing to eat at Waffle House. Food can be comforting and it was probably the only comforting thing at that crazy time in my life. When I think about going to that Waffle House and making small talk with the waitress, the feelings that wash over me are ones of comfort and normalcy. I am very grateful for that because everything else was so chaotic and out of control at that time. Having a regular conversation with a waitress assured me that all could return to normal because they looked at me and saw a normal girl getting a Patty Melt and a Coke. Strangely, it gave me hope.

After eating, I drove to South Dallas to pick up my rent. Frank was able to give me half of it so I could finally relax. The next thing I did was call an attorney. I didn't have a clue what that would cost. I didn't even know if I needed representation, what I needed was advice. He called Rockwall and, as far as he knew, there was not a warrant for my arrest, or at least it was not yet public, but he said they probably had one "in their pocket" and would arrest me, advising me to stay out of Rockwall. He really wouldn't offer more advice until I could retain him, for a cost of $5,000, which I did not have. I had about $600 on me, but I needed that to keep my room and to live on. Plus as a drug addict and I wanted some drugs. I gave him $200 as a down payment and left, not sure what to do or where to go.

My next stop, sadly enough, was to see my dealer. I was nervous because I didn't know if they knew my husband had been arrested. If they did, I didn't think they would sell me any drugs. (It was about me and my needs; the selfish mind of the addict.) They would be scared my husband was going to turn them in. But when I called, it all seemed "normal" and when I went by, I could tell they didn't know anything. I left shortly after to go back to my motel room where I tried to call my kids. Crying, I begged to be able to talk to them, but they wouldn't let me. They kept telling me to turn myself in. I told them I didn't have a warrant, but it didn't matter; I was not allowed any contact. Sadly, I hung up the phone, sat down, and just cried. I was extremely worried about my kids;

they must have been so very scared. I remember the four of us sitting in my car as they described the conversation with the CPS investigator the week prior. I hugged each of them and promised nothing bad was going to happen. I promised it was going to be okay. But my promises were empty because I could not stop the drug abuse. I was too weak and now CPS had come and taken them out of school in front of their friends. It must have been horrible.

Alexis and Sammy were so young; I don't know what they must have thought. Hailey, my oldest and in 6th grade at the time, describes that as the worst moment of her life, how she was crying uncontrollably because her world was rocked to its core. The addiction had such a grip on me because I watched as Hailey withdrew into isolation. My little girl, who was once outgoing and full of life, was slowly withdrawing into a shell, and I did not have the power within me to stop doing drugs. That is what addiction does; it overpowers you and takes control of your life.

I love my children more than anything, but I was helpless to my addiction, too proud and scared to admit I had a problem. And on April 19th, my addiction robbed me of everything that I loved, valued, and held dear in my life. And it was going to get a whole lot worse before it got any better.

It had been a very long weekend and I was basically "on the run." My kids were gone (thankfully CPS turned them over to my husband's parents), my husband was locked up with no chance for bond, and I was too scared to call my Dad. I was all alone in a motel room not knowing what to do. It was the most desperate and alone I think I have ever felt in my life.

I had been calling in sick to work and knew I had to do something because I couldn't continue doing nothing. Finally, I mustered up the courage and called the GISD benefits office. To this day I can't remember who I talked to, but she was an angel sent from God. Crying, I told her I was in a lot of trouble with the police, on drugs, and I didn't know what to do. (As I type this, I am crying so hard because I can still feel the pain, desperation and fear I felt at that time) She told me, in the kindest gentlest voice, to calm down because that is what she was there for. She suggested I check into Baylor Richardson Hospital to be assessed, reminding me that I had insurance that I should utilize. She told me things were going to get better and asked that I please not do anything drastic. I think she was crying too because she was so scared for me and what I might do. She then offered to call my principal and tell him what was happening.

Relief flooded my body because she didn't judge me. She didn't think I was horrible; she just knew I was in trouble and needed help. I needed her and her reaction that day. To be honest, I don't know what I would have done if she had been judgmental. I never thought I would consider suicide because I saw what my brother's suicide did to my family, but I was WITHOUT HOPE that day and I couldn't see a way out. I didn't want people to see the real me and what I had become. I was covered in shame and did not feel I could face anyone. But she looked past all that and treated me with love and respect. I have thought about her often and her impact on my life that day; it was huge. I have always hoped to treat everyone I come into contact with the way she treated me. I fail sometimes, but the memory of the despair I felt that morning is always close to my heart and when she treated me with love and acceptance, it gave me hope. Isn't it amazing how a little kindness and love changed a potentially tragic situation? It takes so little to be loving and kind. I took her advice and drove straight to Baylor Richardson.

I parked my Silver Toyota Camry and took a deep breath. My car was a mess because I had basically been on the run, going from motel to motel. I had not been back to my home since the drug bust, so throughout the weekend I had to buy clothes, personal hygiene products, etc. I had to buy everything because I had walked out of that school on the 19th with only my purse. So I sat in my car, mustering up the courage to walk in to that hospital and say I was a drug addict. I had never admitted that before this day. As I looked through my car, I picked up the plastic baggie that had the traces of Meth I had left and just stared at it. Thoughts began to bombard my mind: "Do the rest of the drugs," "Go ride around and finish what you have, then come back" and to "Throw the drugs away and check into that hospital." Again, I took a deep breath and put the baggie into a paper sack I had from McDonalds and got out of my car. Slowly, I walked to a trash can, looked at the bag one last time, then shoved it into the trash, turning quickly I ran into the emergency room.

Breaking down into tears, I told the lady in the admissions that I was a drug addict and I needed help. I was admitted into the hospital and accessed. I was sent to the fourth floor, which was for patients dealing with substance abuse issues as well as mental problems. I was so scared, but I was also relieved. In a way, I had finally surrendered. I spent three days there. We participated in groups, attended AA meetings, and listened to speakers who came to share their stories. Many of the patients on the floor had severe mental problems and for the first time in a long time, I felt a little hope because my problems didn't seem as severe as some of the people I met there.

After my release I went to stay with my father. Although our relationship was very dysfunctional, I was thankful to have a place to stay. At this point, we were in a waiting game to see if I would be charged along with my husband. I thought there was a good chance I would not be, since I wasn't at home during the arrest, but we just had to wait and see if I was indicted. This experience had a shock value on me and I was certain I would never use drugs again. I thought I should be proactive, so I checked myself into Nexus Recovery, a drug treatment center for women in Dallas, in the hopes of showing the judge that I was addressing my addiction. While at Nexus, I received a call from my attorney saying I was in the paper. I asked if it was the Rockwall paper and he said, "No it was the Dallas Morning News." The headlines read, *Teacher Indicted on Drug Charges, Meth Lab Found in Home.* That is how I — and everyone else — learned about my indictment. And, as I would later learn, the publicity surrounding the case would only make my chances for a light sentence worse. To make matters worse, the paper printed my maiden name in the article, identifying me as "Susan DeFace Washington." Because DeFace is an unusual name, anyone who ever knew me and read that article was certain to know. It was like God was not going to let me hide anymore. All my dirty little secrets were going to come out.

wall parking lot in October. Prosecutors said Mr. Shaw was found later with the trailer and equipment. His attorney could not be reached for comment. Lone Oak Police Chief Miron Klotz said that he had been unaware of the investigation and that Mr. Shaw had resigned a month ago. If convicted, Mr. Shaw could be sentenced to as much as two years in a state jail and fined up to $10,000. Authorities said they expected to issue an arrest warrant next week.

Teacher indicted on drug charge

Meth lab found in home, police say

By Jeff Mosier
Rockwall Bureau

ROCKWALL — A special education teacher at Lakeview Centennial High School in Garland was indicted Wednesday on a charge of manufacturing a controlled substance.

The indictment of Susan Deface Washington, 40, came less than a month after her husband and two other people were arrested at the couple's Rockwall home and charged with the same crime.

Ms. Washington could not be reached. Her attorney, Fred Shelton, said he did not know about the indictment and would not comment. The charge is punishable by two to 20 years in prison.

Reavis Wortham, a Garland school district spokesman, said Ms. Washington would be placed on administrative leave pending the outcome of an investigation. She has been on sick leave since mid-April, he said.

"We'll put a substitute teacher in there for the rest of the school year," Mr. Wortham said.

Ms. Washington had taught in the district since August, he said.

On April 19, Rockwall police were called to Ms. Washington's home in the 1000 block of North Fannin Street about a fight in the front yard. When authorities arrived just after 8:15 a.m., they said, they found a methamphetamine lab and drug paraphernalia in the home.

Police also reported unclean living conditions. Three children, ages 8, 9 and 11, who lived at the house were placed in the custody of their grandparents.

Warren Washington, 41, of Rockwall; Eric Fassoth, 23, of League City, near Galveston; and Courtney Dean, 19, of Webster, near Houston, were arrested and charged with manufacture and delivery of a controlled substance. All three remain in the Rockwall County jail.

Mr. Washington also had outstanding warrants from Rockwall County, Dallas County and The Colony on charges that included evading arrest and violation of probation on a drug possession charge, Rockwall police officials said.

Ms. Washington was not in police custody Wednesday. "We'll probably have an arrest warrant for her on Friday," said Rick Calvert, Rockwall County assistant district attorney.

---

calls for "the peopl States to learn m contributions and Asian/Pacific Ame celebrate the rol played in our natior

I can't think of accomplish this ta: tending Asian Festi

The festival, w from 11 a.m. to 4 p the Annette Strauss 1800 Leonard St., al events celebratin ic American Herita

"This festival is that involves the American communi Patel, chairman o Dallas Asian Amer of Commerce. Asians, there is n and at this one ever will be able to com many different cu time."

LOTTO

WEDNESDAY
8 9 17
19 23 40

Jackpot: **$14 millio**
Winners: **0**
Winning ticket sold
Sat. results: 4 6
Pri
6:6 $10 milli
5:6 $2.6
4:6 $
3:6

Next drawing:
Estimated jackpot

Matthew 10: 26 "But don't be afraid of those who threaten you. For the time is coming when everything that is covered will be revealed, and all that is secret will be made known to all."

My lawyer made a plea and I was sent to a six month rehab in Overton, Texas, and received 10 years adjudicated probation. The time in rehab was good for me; it gave me opportunities to reflect on my life and all the pain I had experienced. To be honest, I liked rehab and got along well there. There was a "phase" system in rehab and I made it through each phase with no problems.

After graduating from rehab, I went to stay with my father again. This was not a good idea. Our relationship was not healthy; and he is an active alcoholic. I was also reunited with my children at this time; and they came to live with us. My dad had a beautiful home. The kids could go to the yacht club and swim, but, as I had learned as a child, material things do not make you happy.

Despite the pleasant physical surroundings, my dad was very critical of me. When he was drunk, he was verbally abusive. He would have a glass full of vodka in his hand, look at me with disgust and throw it in my face. He would say, "I wish you would have died instead of Kathey because she would have never embarrassed and humiliated me the way that you have."

At the time, I believed I deserved that treatment with all my heart. It just compounded the shame and condemnation I already felt about myself. Trying to find work after rehab was also difficult. Part of that problem was pride, with thoughts like "I have a college education, I am not going to work there," when faced with job prospects in food service or retail.

At the time, I was pretty clueless about how this felony was going to affect my life. I called about a potential job with Terrell ISD; the school was desperate for a substitute teacher for one very disruptive student. They told me to show up the next day and we could "take care of paper work later." Despite my efforts to tell them about the felony, they were desperate to fill the position and assured me that it could be discussed at a later time. The optimistic person that I am took that as a sign from God that I was going to start my new position and be so wonderful at it, that they would overlook my 2nd degree felony conviction of manufacturing Meth! (What alternate universe was I living in???)

After about three or four weeks of working, I finally got to see an assistant superintendent. (I was really trying to be honest and do the right thing.) I will never forget sitting across his desk and describing what had happened. He looked me in the eye and said he didn't think it would be a problem. I returned to the classroom with my one student, thinking all was going to be fine. Later that afternoon, the principal and other administrators came to the door and escorted me to the principal's office. They let me know that I needed to leave the premises; and they would not need my services anymore. This was one of the most humiliating experiences of my life. Again, shame and self-loathing washed all over me. Later, I learned that I would probably not teach again and would lose my teaching certificate because of the choices I had made. That news was heartbreaking because I had worked so hard to get my degree. I loved teaching. Hopelessness set in and I relapsed on Meth.

Within a week I was back to using every day, and using more than I had before. The look on my children's faces as I walked out of the bathroom, after being locked in there for what seemed like hours, breaks my heart. My son Sammy said, "Momma, it makes us think you are using again when you stay gone so long and lock yourself in the bathroom." I lied to them, promised that I wasn't using, but you could read the disbelief all over their sweet broken faces.

Craziness returned to my life with my drug use. I had many near misses with the law and even death, as everything was out of control until I was finally stopped.

It was Sunday May 26, 2002, the day before Memorial Day. I was back to using daily. I had gone to Kilgore, Texas to see a friend from rehab who I had relapsed with. I left to drive back to Rockwall. I needed gas but put it off and ran out in Lindale, Texas off of Interstate 20. I saw no station in sight, so I began to walk when a man in an 18 wheeler pulled over. Excited about help, I approached the truck, but when he opened the door my heart skipped a beat out of fear. He was rough looking as he told me to get in. Even in my altered state, my gut told me I was in trouble. Looking around skittishly, I didn't know what to do. Impatiently he yelled for me get in again just as a DPS officer pulled up to ask if there was a problem. Not sure what to do because I had drugs on me, I was scared of the officer but I was also very scared of the man in the truck, so I told the trooper I ran out of gas and went with him. I was so nervous after getting gas; he asked if he could search my car.

I felt that was going to happen. I had stashed the drugs in the grass on the side of the highway, but I didn't get rid of my pipe and some empty baggies that I used to contain Meth. The officer thought about arresting me since he knew I was on probation, but decided to give a paraphernalia ticket instead. I left shaking with fear, but the next day I got more drugs God saved me that day and tried to warn me with that ticket to get back on the right path, but I chose the path of self-destruction. I'm not sure what would have happened if I got in that truck, but the red flags were flying frantically, and I chose to go with an officer while on probation for manufacturing Meth, high, and with drugs on me, I was so scared. That decision may have very well saved my life. God certainly works in mysterious ways. I'm thankful he intervened that day, although I didn't see the blessing then and the craziness continued!

A few days after my encounter in Lindale Texas, I got pulled over at LBJ and La Prada after leaving my drug dealer's house. It was June 5, 2002. As the policemen went to their car to run my license, I knew I would be searched, so I tried to swallow the drugs I had. It was hard, but I succeeded. I think I eventually swallowed four baggies of Meth, coke, and various pills. Although the baggies got stuck in my throat, I was finally able to swallow them. As they went down, the reality set in that I could OD on all these drugs. I ingested a lot and what I didn't eat resulted in a felony charge. I was really scared because I didn't want to die, but I didn't want to tell the cops I ate the evidence either, so I just remained silent.

As I laid in my cell in the Mesquite City Jail, I just waited to die, but death didn't come and I finally drifted off to sleep. Hours later, I was awakened by officers telling me to get up, that I was being transferred to Dallas County Jail. Not long after being booked into Lew Sterrett, my father bailed me out. As I walked out into the hot Texas sun that June day, I was so thankful to be free, but knew I was in deep trouble and a panic began to rise within me.

My hopes were that my probation officer would not find out about my new charge since it was in Dallas County. I made a vow to quit using drugs and entered an outpatient treatment program at Nexus. That feeble attempt at sobriety lasted about one day, and I began using again. While my children and father thought I was at outpatient treatment, I was driving around aimlessly for hours each day looking for my next high. I was basically on the go all the time, driven by a fear of what would happen, but I just couldn't stop. Each morning I would say, "I will quit tomorrow!" but tomorrow never came. The craziness intensified.

On June 24, 2002, I escaped death once again. It had been a couple of weeks since I got my new possession charge and I was frantic, so scared my probation officer was going to find out, that I stayed away from home as much as possible. I was feeling hopeless and knew my life was out of control again, but I couldn't stop. I just didn't realize how far gone I was and how dangerous my life was becoming.

By this time it was just me and my Dad at the house in Rockwall. Sammy and Alexis were spending a lot of time at Warner's parents since I was back to using daily. Hailey was in and out between Rockwall and Wylie where their grandparents lived. The weekend before that fateful Monday, I had gone to Kilgore to get high with some friends and get away from Rockwall. It was just crazy times and the problem was, I didn't really know anyone in Kilgore. The people I was acquaintances with were all using very heavily, no one really had a home or a place for me to stay. So I was going from place to place, just jumping around. I had been up for days and was running out of money, so I knew I needed to get back to Rockwall. After driving around alone all Sunday night, I decided to start the drive back home early Monday morning. The biggest problem was that I was out of dope and very tired.

I started going west on I-20 about 8:30 or so that morning and was barely able to keep my eyes open. Honestly, I don't recall the drive other than nodding off and shaking myself awake occasionally. The next thing I remember was waking up as I ran off the road into a concrete culvert, shaking and wide awake now due to the impact. I emerged from my car to investigate the damage, the front end of my car was smashed and my two front tires were flat and damaged. I knew the car was not drivable. Amazingly, I was not hurt at all because, from the looks of the car, I should have been injured. No one noticed me or the car. There wasn't much traffic going west that Monday morning. I felt invisible. Taking a quick look at the clock in my car, I noticed it was about 9:40 or 9:45. I climbed up the culvert trying to figure out what to do. My mind was not clear and I didn't have anyone to call, so I began to walk. Looking across I-20, I saw a gas station/restaurant and decided to run over there to get some cigarettes and something to eat and drink. Then I would make my plan.

As I ran across the west bound lanes of I-20, I stopped in the grassy median of the east and west bound lanes. I noticed there was a lot of traffic backed up heading east and wondered what was happening. As I ran across the east bound lanes between cars not moving, I heard the sound of helicopters above. Meth tends to make you very paranoid and delusional, so I wasn't sure if the helicopters were real or if I was having hallucinations. I just knew I was scared and wanted to get in the station and splash water on my face to try and gather my thoughts and distinguish what was real and what was an illusion. As I ran into the restroom, I shivered slightly as I looked in the mirror. I looked horrible and worn out. I was somewhat surprised that my appearance went downhill so fast. I had only been using again for about a month, before that I had over a year clean, but I looked just as ragged as I had when we got busted the year before. I cupped water in my hand from the faucet, throwing it on my face, and wet my hair in the sink, attempting to clean up. Looking in the mirror one more time, a tear rolled down my cheek because the reflection looking back at me was obviously a drug addict. I hated who I had become. I pushed those feelings down, took a deep breath and went out to buy something. It was then that I heard the sound of sirens and more helicopters.

Knowing this was not my imagination; I walked out of the store and saw there was no movement at all on I-20 east. Looking up I saw that some of the helicopters were from hospitals and some were from Dallas news stations. Fire trucks, highway patrol, and ambulances were driving in the grass on the median I had just run across trying to make it through the traffic. Afraid and stunned by what I was witnessing, I asked someone in the parking lot if they knew what happened. They said they weren't sure. As a policeman pulled into the station, I got very paranoid because I was on drugs. I didn't have any left, but I did have paraphernalia on me. To be honest, I was freaking out because on some level I thought they could be looking for me, because my probation officer had found out about my new charge, issued a warrant and sent the Rockwall Sheriff's department to arrest me. That is what Meth does; it is just unbelievable how your mind runs crazy. I know of tragic things that have happened when people were in a paranoid delusion due to Meth.

I wanted to get away from the cops so I decided to run back to my car and charge my phone. As I ran to it, I noticed more helicopters hovering overhead. Whatever happened was really bad and was really close. Although my car was not drivable, I could start it. That was not the best idea, but I wasn't thinking clearly and needed to get the charge on my phone up so I could call to see if someone could help me, and maybe find out what was going on. With all the news helicopters, I was sure there was probably a broadcast. All I knew is something horrible happened because of all the emergency vehicles I was seeing. I knew that it probably happened at about the same time as I fell asleep at the wheel and went off the road. Shaking, I got in my car, turned the key, and plugged my phone in. I rested my head back and closed my eyes, wondering how on earth I was going to get myself out of this mess, not realizing how lucky I was to be alive, because across that highway, a bus carrying a group of teenagers to church camp crashed into a concrete pillar killing five people. The speculation was the driver fell asleep at the wheel. As I thought about it later, I realized that the bus crash and my crash happened about the same time. We had probably passed each other. I would run off into a culvert and walk away without a scratch and the bus would hit a concrete pillar killing four innocent teenagers and the driver. For some reason, God spared my life; and it didn't seem fair at all. The timing of these two incidents was unbelievable.

There was no one to call to help me. I was too scared to call my dad, plus I had totaled one of his cars, so he was the last person I wanted to see. I began to walk west on I-20, hoping to get to Terrell. Finally, after awhile, a pickup truck pulled over and gave me a ride. I was too tired to even be scared. Once in Terrell, I called a "drug" friend and asked her to come get me. I told her that if she did, I would get her some Meth. She came to pick me up then took me back to Rockwall.

I honestly can't remember what I told my father about the car, but I lied and he believed it. Unbeknownst to me, my father's life was spiraling out of control along with mine; and we were about to hit bottom so hard that we couldn't run anymore.

The next couple of weeks are a drug hazed memory filled with more insanity. After totaling one car, the next car I was using was stolen by Meth cooks leaving me stranded in Kilgore. I was on the run because I learned my father called my probation officer and told her I had a new charge, so she was looking for me. After the very scary Meth cooks stole my car, I was too scared to call the police, so I kept trying to find them. But the problem was, I was in a town where I knew no one, only a few drug addicts that could have cared less about me or my car, especially since I didn't have any drugs. One girl, who I had been in rehab with, hit me in the face with her fist because she thought I stole her belongings. As blood poured out of my nose, I began to cry and just wanted to get home. The problem was, I had no money and now no car.

Finally, I was able to get a bus ticket to Terrell at the Greyhound station. As the bus pulled out of Kilgore, I sighed with relief that I was getting out of the drug induced crazy world that I had gotten myself into. It was over, I couldn't run anymore. Weary with defeat, I dozed off for most of the trip.

When I walked into my dad's house, I immediately knew something was terribly wrong with him. He could barely hold his head up and was coughing horribly. His skin had a grayish tint; and I feared he was very ill. He would not go to the doctor. Although I pleaded with him, he was adamant about not going. So he sat in his chair, smoked cigarettes, and drank vodka for two days. During that time, I was preparing for my probation meeting on Thursday July 18, hoping she would not revoke me for my new charge. On Wednesday the 17th, I forced my dad to go with me to the hospital. He looked so bad; plus I was so scared that when I went to probation on Thursday, I might be arrested. If I was arrested, I was scared he would just die alone in that house. As I said before, it was just me and him. He was immediately admitted with double pneumonia. He almost died, and would have died if he didn't get care. On July 18th I walked into my probation meeting and was immediately arrested with no bond.

Rockwall County Jail Mug Shot

CHAPTER 7

Sometimes What Seems Like Surrender Isn't Surrender At All

Sometimes what seems like surrender isn't surrender at all. It's about what's going on in our hearts. About seeing clearly how life is and accepting it and being true to it, whatever the pain, because the pain of not being true to it is far, far greater.
— Horse Whisperer

My life in Rockwall County Jail was hard at first, but I slowly accepted my fate and served my time. Rockwall had not had a woman trustee (a trustee is a well-behaved and trustworthy convict to whom special privileges are granted) in about ten years and they decided to have one again. All the inmates, including myself, were filling out applications for the job. I was chosen for this coveted position. How sad that I really felt honored to be chosen, but I was proud of my new job. The perks that came along with being a trusty were: smoking cigarettes, a cell by yourself, an extra blanket and pillow, more food, a remote control for the TV, using a free phone one time a day, and the list went on. (The things you appreciate in jail are quite different than what you appreciate in the free world.) My duties as trustee were to do the women inmates' laundry and prepare mop buckets for the cells. Life in Rockwall County settled into a routine. I enjoyed spending time with the guards and nurse there. Some guards were studying for their college entrance exams; and I tutored them. My hopes were to be able to stay in the county jail and do my time there, but no one knew if that would happen.

One thing I learned in jail is criminals lie! It shouldn't be that shocking that criminals lie, but they got me every time. I couldn't believe that I trusted what they said!

While I wasn't sure where I might do my time, "not knowing" when I was going to leave was the hardest part. When you were called to leave, guards would wake you up at three in the morning and tell you to pack your things because, "You were pulling chain." (I learned all kinds of interesting phrases during my unfortunate incarceration, for instance, the first time someone told me I was going to pull chain, I went into my cell and started crying. One of my favorite guards came in asking me what was wrong. I told her that I didn't want to have to pull chains, that it sounded really hard. She started laughing hysterically saying that I wasn't going to literally pull chains. The term meant you were leaving the county jail for prison. I was so very relieved, I started to laugh! And that was just the first prison lingo that I learned. There would be so much more during this crazy experience.)

Summer turned into fall and then winter came at the Rockwall County Jail. With my daily chores as the only female trustee, I had almost forgotten that I could be called to "pull chain" any day because I had been there so long. It was also nice because my children could visit me once a week as they lived so close. Eventually, it was easy to sleep at night because I had quit worrying about leaving and really thought I might get to stay in Rockwall. However, on November 13th at three in the morning, the guard woke me up, told me to pack my things, that I was pulling chain. I was shocked, dismayed, and terrified about would happen next, because I didn't have a clue. I knew not to believe what my inmate friends told me.

The journey to and through prison was quite an adventure, starting with the drive from Rockwall. The officer who transported me to the Woodman Unit in Gatesville Women's Prison was very nice, and told me I could smoke as many cigarettes as I wanted because I wouldn't be able to smoke in prison. So as we drove off, I lit one up and continued to smoke the whole way there. We arrived at Woodman, which is a diagnostic unit, around 11 in the morning. As we pulled through gates and fences lined with barbed wire, I saw other cars from different counties bringing their prisoners. I was so scared; I didn't want the Rockwall Sheriff to leave me. He told me it was going to be okay, that he had to go back home. I am surprised I didn't grab hold of him, but I just sadly waved as he walked away and got in his car. The rest of that day was a blur of tests, being measured, throwing all of our personal items away except one Bible, getting clothes, shoes, I.D. badges, etc.

TDCJ Offender Badge

It was the longest day ever. That evening around 8 or 9, we were finally taken to our dorms. The dorm held about 100 women, all just arriving to prison. The next days would be intellectual tests, medical tests, and skill tests to see what kind of job might be best for each of us. One of the most demeaning, awful things was that I had no personal hygiene products. I was handed two bars of blue lye soap to clean everything with; and it was supposed to last for a while. The only way you could get shampoo, toothpaste or regular soap was to have money on your commissary. If you were indigent, you could receive hygiene products, but the process of being declared indigent could take weeks and maybe months.

As I settled into my bunk, I had no problem falling asleep that first night. The day had been so exhausting. Sometime in the middle of the night, I woke up, not sure where I was. Sitting up in my bunk, looking around at all the inmates sleeping, I thought, *"How on earth did I end up here? Where did it all go so terribly wrong?"* There were no answers to my questions. God, however, would answer those questions later.

My time at Woodman was only a few weeks. I passed all the academic tests with a "college +" rating and was declared completely healthy. The next step was waiting to see where we went next. Time was spent playing games, usually scrabble, reading, and visiting with other inmates. It seemed like most of the inmates I was with at that point were drug offenders like me. Right after Thanksgiving, the call came for 50 of us to get up and pack our things because we were pulling chain. My next stop was Dawson State Jail in Dallas, Texas. A state jail is for criminals with a state jail felony (their time could be from about six months to two years; and they serve every day of their time), but we were going there waiting for room to open up on our regular units. We were sent to a dorm on the seventh floor and given blue jump suits to distinguish us from the other female offender doing time there. (All girls in blue had 1st, 2nd or 3rd degree felonies and were serving time of 2+ years with a chance for parole.)

Dawson reminded me a lot of a county jail. It is a high rise and you cannot go outside, so you don't get any fresh air. Adjusting to a new dorm and new people is never easy, but I was with some of the girls I had met at Woodman, so there was some familiarity which made me feel more comfortable. Again, I spent my time reading, talking with inmates and going to various church services. The best thing about Dawson was the visits from my family; they could come each weekend because it was not too far from Wylie. My kids were doing well and we were lucky that my husband's parents and sister had stepped in to provide a stable home for them. The worst thing about Dawson was the food and commissary; you just didn't get what you ordered. I know it seems silly, but commissary made prison bearable for me. When we didn't get what we ordered, there was nothing we could do about it. Christmas was bittersweet that year, being locked up, away from my family, but I was to a point of acceptance, hoping to make parole as soon as possible.

After the New Year passed, the call came again to pack up. This time we were going to our unit. There was some excitement among the women because we knew we were about to be settled in for a while and given a job to do. Our destination was the Hilltop Unit in Gatesville. The bus trips we took to various destinations were very uncomfortable because we were always handcuffed and our legs shackled, so it was great to arrive and get off the bus. The first thing we did after arriving at Hilltop was to get in line and talk to a commanding officer who would give us a job. I was 41 at the time; and had been told by my "inmate friends" that if you were over 40, you would not have to be on the Hoe Squad. That was such a relief, because on the Hoe Squad, you are shackled together and had to hoe the ground all day long. The girl who was ahead of me in line was also over 40 and she was as relieved as I was.

Girls would walk in, and then come out with a job. Many of the jobs were in laundry, at the sewing factory, the dreaded Hoe squad, and in the cafeteria. Some went straight to the trustee camp where they worked on the various farms. It was my friend's turn to go in and I was nervous for her, hoping she would get a job she could tolerate. When she came out, she was crying, so I asked her what was wrong. She told me she got placed on the Hoe Squad. I was shocked because we were told no one over 40 was put on the Hoe Squad, but then I remembered our source of the information: inmates!!! Where I had been nervous before, now fear entered my body. I walked into the office and approached the commanding officer who was reading my file. She stopped and looked up at me and said, "You are way too smart to be here, what happened?" I didn't think she really wanted to hear my whole story and that the question was more rhetorical, so I just shrugged and said I messed up. She started talking with another officer and then told me there was a job in the library. Since I had done so well on the tests with a college + education, she thought I could probably alphabetize. So I was to be a librarian! As I left, everyone asked what job I was assigned. One girl pulled me aside to warn me, because that was a coveted job. I decided to keep it to myself, but secretly I was thrilled not to be on the Hoe Squad.

The next thing we did was go to the chow hall and have lunch. The food was 100% better than it was at Dawson. After lunch, we were sent to our dorms to unpack. This is where I got separated from all my "friends." Another change was taking place. That is one thing about prison; you have to learn to adjust to change and basically always being told what to do.

I was assigned to a dorm called the "Big Timer." I didn't know what that meant. There was a popular rap group at the time called Big Tymers, so I thought it might be a dorm that liked rap music. I just wasn't sure. Walking into the dorm was nerve-wracking because I was alone and didn't know anyone. The guard showed me my bunk and I started unpacking. I had accepted my fate and, because by nature I am a pretty laid back, friendly girl, I decided to start introducing myself to my new "roommates." There were probably 50 of us in the dorm and we each had a bed with a small storage area. As I approached a fellow inmate, I told her, "Hi, my name is Susan and I am a drug offender with a two year sentence." I asked her what she had done to get to prison. She snarled at me and told me she had killed her kids and was doing life. Disbelief and shock are the only ways I can describe my reaction. Up to that point, I had only seen drug offenders.

Another inmate approached me and told me to come over because she had some advice for me. I decided to listen to her. She told me the dorm was called the Big Timer dorm because most everyone was doing "big time" and I didn't need to be talking about "my little two-year sentence" because they would just try to get me in trouble. She then started pointing to various women telling me their crimes: one had decapitated her parents and tried to sew the heads on the other body; another had microwaved her baby and tried to feed it to her husband; one had been a school teacher in Richardson and killed her two sons after losing them in a custody battle; and one had killed someone who had abused her kids. They all were doing life with no chance for parole for a very long time. I was mortified! Quickly I ran up to the guard and explained that there had been a huge mistake, that I was a very, very, very (I was trying to get my point across) NON-VIOLENT drug offender. (I mean, I have never even got in a physical fight with anyone.) He looked at me and said it didn't matter, there had been no mistake.

Now I was scared. I was living in a dorm with a bunch of murderers and I didn't see much hope and compassion in their eyes. Several were suffering from severe mental illness, you could see it in their eyes and behavior, (the one who decapitated her parents, for example) and some were simply evil (the one who microwaved her baby). My plan was to stay on my bunk and read; thank God I got to work in the library. My bunk was also right by the guard, so that gave me some comfort that I might not be murdered in the middle of the night. My day went like this: 4:00 a.m., get clothes at the laundry;

5:00 a.m., breakfast was served in the chow hall; school started at 8:00 so we would walk to the library around 7:45 and pick up the books; 11:00 lunch then back to work. At 4:00, work was over and we went back to our dorm. Supper was served at about 5:30 or 6:00; 7:00 we went back to the library to work as the dorms came to check out books; 8:00 to 10:00 were times for showers. We did not have showers in the dorm, there was one room with about 100 showers and we went with our dorm mates. There was no privacy at all, just 100 showerheads descending from the ceiling. If you started out shy in prison, you would get over it fast because whether it was showering or being searched, people always saw you completely undressed!

Although I liked Hilltop a lot better than Dawson because I could go outside, and the food and commissary were better, my family couldn't visit as much and we could not talk on the phone. The guards said we would get phone privileges after being on the unit six months; and at that point, we would get one five-minute call. The hardest part for me was the lack of communication with the outside world. We could only communicate by mail; and we live in a society where we are used to instant communication. But I had settled into my life at Hilltop, still hoping for parole. But without much communication, I just didn't know anything.

Most my time in prison was spent reading on my bunk, but occasionally I would wander to the TV room where the inmates could play board games or watch TV. The most popular game was Scrabble and one day I decided to sit in and play. The girls I was playing against were some of the murderers I had mentioned earlier. One took her turn and laid out a word that was not a word. Being a former educator, I decided to point that out to her as delicately as possible. After telling her the letters she played did not make a word, she yelled at me and said, "It is a word!" Startled by her defensiveness and anger I said, "Okay, okay, it's a word." In my opinion, if a murderer says a word is a word, it is! From then on, anything went in Scrabble and I never pointed out incorrect words again.

The other thing that amazed me in prison was how the inmates cooked with their coffee pots that they bought at commissary. They would make casseroles, enchiladas, and even cheesecake. It was all surprisingly good. I told them they needed to write a cookbook. I never mastered coffee pot cooking, but that isn't surprising because I couldn't cook in the free world either.

By nature I am a compliant person and when I ended up in prison, I was not going to break any rules because I knew it was by small compromises that I ended up there in the first place. I had pushed boundaries a little bit at a time, until I had completely changed a core value. There was one instance where I did break the rules; and I just felt I had to. Commissary made prison bearable; I can't imagine doing time without it. It was the only treat there was. Many girls I met didn't have money for commissary. I felt so sad for them. It was against the rules to share your commissary, you could get charged with an extra case and have your sentence extended, but in this instance, I took a chance and bought small items for other inmates. It was very rewarding to see the smile on their faces when I asked them if I could get them something when I went to the store. Their reaction when I actually brought them something was priceless. It still warms my heart. So I know I broke a rule, but I wanted them to feel better. It wasn't right, but I never got in trouble for it and, in my opinion, it was worth it.

One day, as I was walking from school to the chow hall, I heard some girls calling, "Mrs. Washington, Mrs. Washington." My first reaction was, "this is strange because, in prison, I am only referred to as Offender Washington 1130254." That is not only how you are addressed, but how you would identify yourself if asked. So I paused as I heard those words, "Mrs. Washington," trying to think when in my life I had ever been called that, as most people call me Susan. Then, slowly, the light came on in my head and I turned to see two of my former students from Amarillo. I was shocked and embarrassed, but they weren't. They ran over to me (which you aren't supposed to do; you are supposed to stay on the line when you walk, so they were making me nervous) laughing and saying "hi." They hated for me to see them in there because I had been one of their favorite teachers. I told them not to worry about it, and oddly enough, they never even asked why I was there. I said it was okay and told them they needed to comply with the rules in prison better than they did with the rules in school. To be honest, I don't know if they took my advice, but I doubt it. I didn't run into them again. That experience really showed me God's sense of humor because, although I was extremely embarrassed, I knew I would really be able to laugh about it one day. . and I am able to laugh about it now. Again, God wasn't letting me hide anything; everything was going to be exposed.

Not long after running into my students, I was in for another surprise. When I arrived at my dorm after lunch one day, I was told to pack my things because I was pulling chain to Trusty Camp. Trusty Camp was supposed to be nicer, offer better food and more freedom, so I was somewhat excited. However, what was most important to me was my library job, so again I asked my "inmate friends" (because really there is no one else to ask, guards don't really talk to you) if I would get to keep my job. My friends assured me I would, that a bus would just bring me to the school each morning. I was so relieved because they seemed to really know what they were talking about (and certainly the odds were in my favor since everything else they told me had been wrong; surely they had to be right once). I was soon on the bus to Trusty Camp and assigned my bunk. I ran into some of the women that I met at the beginning of my sentence so that was nice. While the camp was nice enough, that was of little importance because I didn't want to socialize with anyone. I typically stayed on my bunk and read books so the extra freedom was not much of an incentive, but again, my friends assured me that I could keep my library job. Although I wanted to believe them with all my heart, something deep within me told me that was not the truth.

Later I was called to the guard and told that I had been assigned a new job. My face dropped, but I had to make the best of it because I had no choice in the matter. I was then told I would be "slopping the pigs." Really!? This was the worst news I had since I arrived at prison. . and remember my first roommates were murderers! I don't know why slopping the pigs was supposedly better than working in the library, but I was just crushed. The pre-pig slopping routine was humiliating: we woke up each morning and had to line up for the guards; completely undress; squat and cough; redress, get on a bus and drive to the slabs. There we put on rubber suits and boots so we could wade through the waste and clean the water, slabs, and food troughs. The smell was horrendous and since we were the trusted trustee's, the guards just dropped us off.

Again, I am a very compliant person and do what I am supposed to do (other than commit a couple of felonies here and there), but this is not true for a lot criminals. Some (most even) have a tendency to rebel and some are quite lazy. So once the guards would leave, a lot of the inmates would start whining and complaining, then go sit down. Well I just wanted to get the job done and over with, but there was not much I could do to make them work. I could not be a snitch — that would have threatened my safety — so the few of us who would work did most the work and the others just whined. We took a break for lunch and finally returned to our unit where again had to completely undress, squat, cough and redress. (Anytime we left or returned to the unit, we repeated this routine, so we undressed, squatted, and coughed AT LEAST four times a day in front of a line of guards.) This was the grossest, most humbling act I have ever had to do, but I did learn from it. After feeding and watering the pigs, we would then return to our unit where we would have the rest of the day free. I stayed on my bunk and read, longing for my days at the library with less freedom. And less pig shit.

One day in May, I was called again to pack my bags because I had a bench warrant to Dallas. I had to take care of the charges that had revoked my probation. At this point, I was serving time for the revocation and had not addressed the new possession charge. To be honest, I was pretty happy because I hated working with the pigs. I arrived at Lew Sterrett, the Dallas County jail, and started the long process of going to my "pod."

Of all the jails that I have been to, Dallas County is by far the worst. The food is awful and just the process to get to your cell takes 24-48 hours, where you are stuffed in cells with other inmates. I entered my first holding cell and there were about 25 women crammed in the very small space. It was around 11 in the morning, so many of them were sobering up from being arrested the night before and some were still passed out, sprawled on the floor. As I walked into the cell, some girls stopped talking and looked me over. When you leave prison, you leave your whites and are issued mismatched scrubs, but I was wearing them with my TDCJ work boots, which I was allowed to do since I had purchased them. My outfit made me stand out. Don't get me wrong, no one mistook me for a nurse or doctor! One particularly scary-looking girl with a tattoo on her neck that read "fuck the police" was staring at me; and I was very frightened. Then she said, "You're from TDC aren't you?" I nodded yes and her sneering look changed to one of admiration. She made some girls move so I could sit on the bench by her. The other girls looked at me with fear since I was a convict from prison. I wasn't sure how to act and was really shocked anyone would ever be frightened of me, but I spent my time talking to my new tattooed friend (because I was scared not to), who had been to prison numerous times (and was probably on her way back) trying to keep up the farce that I was some tough girl which, obviously, is so far from the truth. It was crazy that I received respect because I was from prison.

I finally arrived to my pod about a day and a half later and settled in. The reaction I received from the inmates in the pod was similar to the holding cell. There was one leader who had just come from state jail that ran the pod with intimidation and fear. When I walked in with my commissary bag, which was obviously from prison, the leader eagerly greeted me and had me sit at her table because I was from TDCJ. While it was just crazy, I went along with it, happy that the scary leaders respected me and my crimes, and laughing inside because the other girls were scared of me! *Because I was from prison!!!*

In county lock-up, the food is awful. Each day for lunch, I got a bologna sandwich, but the bologna had a disgusting green tint. I thanked God for commissary. I spent one month in Dallas, went to court, plead guilty, and got "time served." I was happy to have that charge resolved. The nice thing about being in Dallas was visits from my family and, believe it or not, air conditionings, as state prisons, even in our relentless Texas heat, are not air conditioned.

It was in Dallas that I learned I would be paroled on June 14. Now my hopes to stay in Dallas and be paroled from here, instead of having to return to prison, might be realistic. Then I wouldn't have to do that whole process of pulling chain, being handcuffed and shackled on the bus, getting admitted to prison yet again. I was so very tired of that. But alas, my wishes did not come true. One morning at about 1 o'clock I was told to pack my things. I was "pulling chain" again. I took a deep breath and did what I was told.

My first stop was Woodman again but thankfully, the process went very fast because I had just been through it before and, as a result, was only there one night. I then was sent to the Gatesville unit and was put in a cell. This was a waiting time and was very uncomfortable because I was in a small cell by myself, and never got to leave. My meals were even brought to me there. To this day, I don't understand what that was about. At the time, no one talked to me. All I knew is that I was supposed to parole soon, but I wasn't clear if it was truly going to happen. As with anything, the waiting is the hardest part. Friday arrived and I knew they were calling girls that were paroling out. A guard walked by my cell. I asked her if I was on the list and she told me "no." I was heartbroken because I knew then that I would have to stay through the weekend in that small cell by myself. Later, the same guard came up to my cell and said she had just got word that I was on the list. I was so very excited! I was getting out of prison that day! I can't describe the happiness I felt. I had been locked up a year and I couldn't believe I was about to be free.

Of course there is as long of a process to get out of prison as there is to get in, but I got through it and we were ready to leave. When you get out on parole, you are issued a $50 check and a bus ticket. We drove to the bank, cashed our checks; and then they took five of us to the local bus station. The five of us did not know each other at all, but we became fast friends. We were all extremely excited to get out. Once we were at the station, we checked the schedule to see when the bus would be leaving for our various destinations. We all had hours before departure, so we decided to walk around Killeen. Again, the attire we were issued was mismatched scrubs so it was obvious we had just been released from prison, especially in Killeen, where prisoners are released daily. Although that embarrassed me, it really didn't dampen my spirits. I was so thrilled to be out.

The first place I went was to a grocery store to buy some real shampoo and cigarettes. I then ran into a public bathroom and washed my hair in a sink. What a treat! I can't describe how happy I was to wash my hair with real shampoo. I then smoked cigarettes. I really can't believe I did that since I hadn't smoked for so long, but I did. At least I would quit for good not too long after that. Next we went to Burger King; and it was so nice to eat a real hamburger. The only meat you get in prison is pork; the pork from the pigs that we raised when I was a pig farmer. (Interesting fact: Texas Prisons are self-supporting, which is pretty cool. The pigs we raised and then slaughtered provided meat; the Hoe Squad raised cabbage and vegetables; and the sewing factory sewed all the whites and coats. Everything prisoners need was done in prison.)

Finally, my husband arrived to pick me up in Killeen and we drove back to Dallas. The first place I had him stop was Starbucks, so I could get a French Vanilla Frappuccino. Then I changed into some real clothes and threw the scrubs and my TDCJ boots in the trash. It was so thrilling to be free, just to be able to walk where I wanted, to use the bathroom alone behind a closed door, take a shower by myself, be called Susan, not Offender # Washington. This list could go on and on. The lack of freedom has such an impact that it is hard to explain. I had many fears about prison that never happened, but the worst thing about it was the loss of freedom in every sense of the word; being treated as less than human. But I didn't have to think about that anymore, I was free!

It was a nice drive back to Wylie with my husband. We had been through so much and hadn't seen each other in two years, but we had both made it. He was working for Albertsons and had found an old trailer for us to rent. Finding a place to live was a challenge because we were now both convicted felons and many places will not lease or rent to felons. He had saved a lot of money and was able to pay eight months' rent in advance for the trailer. As felons, that was the only way we were able to rent it. As we drove down his parent's street to pick up our kids, I could hardly contain my excitement. The kids ran out of the house as we pulled up and parked. It was one of the most special moments in my life. Looking into their hopeful faces, my prayer was not to let them down again. They had been through so much with the first arrest and then my relapse. I knew I had to rebuild trust with them. Our family dynamics were so different now: Warner was the anchor and the kids looked to him for everything, where in the past I had been their rock. Initially, I felt like an outsider watching them interact, but I knew it would only take time for them to get to know and trust me again. I had really let them down and I vowed to myself and God not to let that happen again. I knew there would be a time that I disappointed them; that is a part of life, but my vow was to stay clean and out of trouble. We left his parents' house and drove to our trailer.

One thing that was nice about the trailer is it was out in the country and not in a trailer park. We lived next to the man who owned it and his parents on the outskirts of Wylie. The kids could run and play, so I was very happy about the location. The trailer on the other hand was hard to get used to, it was very run down. I just didn't want anyone to see where I lived. That was really not a problem since I had not had contact with any of my friends for a very long time. When you spiral into a drug addiction, you usually distance yourself from your friends who don't use drugs and that had happened in my life. So I was really not in relationship with anyone at all other than my kids; and I was so thankful to be back with them.

Next, as a parolee in the state of Texas, I had to go see my parole officer in Garland. I had one day to show up or I would be in trouble, so on Monday I reported to parole. It was at this time I had the monitor put on my leg. To be honest, I was a little offended that I had to wear one, no one else that I was released with had to wear a leg monitor and most of them had been to prison multiple times. I didn't really understand why I had to be on house arrest, but I didn't really care because even the trailer, as much as I hated it, was better than prison. It was air conditioned. My parole officer informed me that I had to wear the monitor because of the publicity in my case. No one wanted to be accused of letting the teacher off easy, but it was almost like reverse discrimination to me at the time. I got more severe consequences because I was a teacher. Again I didn't really care because I was free and my "inmate friends" told me that wearing a leg monitor was no big deal. The only rule was you had to be in the house by seven in the evening and couldn't leave until seven the next morning. That didn't sound too bad.

Well, guess what, they were wrong!!! The leg monitor was so very strict. I reported to parole every two weeks and had to have a detailed schedule prepared if I wanted to leave the house at all. Honestly, I could not even walk out on my porch without permission. The only approved places to go were job interviews, AA or NA meetings, and church. My organizational skills were not keen enough for me to be able to schedule two weeks of activity, so I just stayed home most all the time. In retrospect, this was very good for me because in the past I always felt I had to be on the go, never being still. My kids spent that summer going to a program called the Wylie Wave and I stayed at home. The program was great for my kids; and it was good for me to adjust to my new life in the trailer. Looking back, this was a time I cherished because even though we had no money, we really enjoyed our time as a family. We spent time playing board games, watching movies together, and just being with each other. It is hard to explain, but when you hit rock bottom, you truly learn to appreciate the little things in life. My kids were so happy, but you could still tell they didn't trust me yet. I just wanted them to feel safe.

September came and I was released from the leg monitor. That was great, although there really wasn't anything to do. I didn't have a job, my license was suspended until my birthday, and I had no friends, so I still spent my days alone in the trailer while the kids were at school. It was during this time I could go visit my dad, he had lost his beautiful home and a business he spent years building because of his alcoholism; and he was not doing very well. I had asked permission from my parole officer to go visit him, but was told the state of Texas could care less about the health of my father. During phone conversations, I knew he wasn't doing well; he always sounded drunk and would tell me he just wanted to die. The next time Warner was off work, we drove to Seagoville where he was living in his old business building that was about to be foreclosed on. We stopped at the grocery store so I could cook him his favorite dish. When we arrived at his office/home, the situation was worse than I thought. He was not able to get up and go to the bathroom, so he was soiled. His dogs had not been let out, so there was waste and urine everywhere. It was just awful and I hated seeing him that way. He was so drunk; it took me back to the memories of my mom. I cleaned and cooked him a meal, but was not sure what else to do. We left that day and I was so concerned because the situation seemed so dangerous with him smoking cigarettes constantly, and being drunk, but he was a grown man and did not want to leave. The next week he called a friend of his who was a dentist and asked for a prescription of pain killers so he could kill himself. We then decided to have him arrested and sent to Green Oaks for an assessment; and to detox. They were able to arrest him since he was considered a danger to himself. This was just so tragic because the ambulance drivers told me they remembered what a wonderful man my father was, and how successful his business had become. He sponsored teams, gave back to the community and helped anyone in need. It broke my heart that they had to fight him to get him in the ambulance. He was screaming that he just wanted to die, in soiled clothes, and virtually all alone. Every relationship he had was broken because of his alcoholism. I was all he had. In his eyes, that wasn't much, but I vowed just to do the best I could to be there for my father.

The detox was awful, as it always is, but I was prepared for that because I had been through it with mother so many times. During his hospitalization, his business was foreclosed on, so he had nowhere to live, and no money. He was destitute. Luckily he had social security and a social worker got him into a nursing home in Wylie. This was good, so I could visit him. It seemed as if things were falling into place for me. I was happy he was near and would be looked after.

CHAPTER 8

Walk Awhile In My Shoes

Remember that I'm Human. Before you judge me or decide how you'll deal with me, walk awhile in my shoes. If you do, I think you'll find with more understanding we can meet in the middle and walk the rest of the way together."
— *Eric Harvey and Steve Ventura:*
Walk Awhile in My Shoes

December of 2003 came and that was the time I would be able to get my driver's license reinstated, plus I had finished all the classes required by my parole officer. I didn't mind going to see my parole officer at all because I was clean. It is amazing how much easier probation and parole are if you just stay clean and do what you are supposed to do. On December 19th, 2003, I was driven to the DMV to get my license reinstated. It was an exciting day, but I was a nervous wreck thinking they were going to run my number and I would have some old ticket that I didn't remember, and get arrested. My heart was beating wildly. I was really terrified wanting to turn around and go home, but it all went smoothly and I got my license back. So I could check that off my list.

The next thing I needed to check into was finding a job. Where I had pride after rehab, I was completely humble after prison. I was willing to work anywhere to help my family (although I was secretly thrilled there were no pig farms in the area). I started applying for jobs. Most of my work experience had been teaching. Many places did not hire me because of my felonies and some because I had no experience. Discouragement was setting in when I decided to go apply at a Dickey's Barbeque that was opening up in Wylie. After dropping off the application, the owner called me in for an interview. I was always, and am to this day, completely honest about my past, because I never want to hide anything ever again. He asked me about teaching, but didn't mention the two felony convictions at all. He then shook my hand and said I was hired. I can't describe how thrilled I was. I left that day with my Dickey's hat and Dickey's shirt excited to restart my career as a drive through cashier. To this day I am so thankful to Bill and Cathy Fowler for giving me the opportunity to show I had changed. My life was slowly but surely turning around, although I was in for more heartache that was beyond my control.

We had settled into a routine and our lives were getting easier. Warner was still at Albertson's and I was working at Dickey's. The kids were doing well in school and our lives were back on track. It seemed like I could take a deep breath and finally relax a little. My daughter Alexis went to a volleyball camp the summer of 2004 and met a girl named Beth Jensen there. Beth had just moved to Wylie from Plano with her parents and younger brother Alex. They became friends and one day Beth's mother, Kerri, called and asked if she could pick Alexis up to come over. I was excited for this relationship, but I was still so embarrassed about the trailer that I told her that I would bring Alexis to her house. Alexis, Hailey, and I drove over to the Jensen's and we all went in their house. Kerri was so nice to us and there was a warm feeling in the home. As Hailey and I left, we looked at each other and said, "I like the Jensen's, they are very nice." The friendship between the girls grew. Then we learned that the Jensen's son, Alex, was the exact same age as Sammy; and we hoped for them to get together.

Summer turned into fall and it was the beginning of the Wylie Football League for 3rd, 4th, and 5th graders. Sammy loved playing football and was picked for a team called the Patriots. We were happily surprised when Alex Jensen was on the same team. He and Sammy became really good friends after that. In the afternoons, they would practice football, go to movies, and hang out. Alex and Beth even invited Sammy and Alexis to their youth group at church; New Hope Christian Church in Wylie. The friendship with this family was very nice, but I was guarded. These were Christians that were highly involved in church and I didn't want them to know that their kids' new friends' parents were recovering drug addicts that had been to prison. I was sure they would reject all of us if they knew that. So I kept them at a distance, always being friendly but never letting anyone too close to learn my horrible secrets. It was a wonderful fall of little league football and the Patriot team made it to the Super Bowl. Although they lost, it was a fun year cheering on our boys.

Christmas came and the Jensens' took a family vacation to Colorado to learn to snow ski. I remember Sammy talking to Alex before they left. They made plans to get together when they returned from Colorado. I was working as many hours as possible at Dickey's, and when I came in one night, Sammy was sitting on the couch looking sad. I asked him what was wrong and he just looked at me with tears in his eyes. Alarmed, I called for Warner who told me he had received a phone call that Alex Jensen had died tragically in a snow skiing accident. He skied into a tree and was declared brain dead the next day.

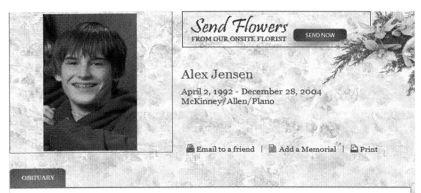

Alex Jensen
April 2, 1992 - December 28, 2004
McKinney/Allen/Plano

OBITUARY

Alex Jensen, age 12 of Wylie, TX, passed away December 28, 2004 in Denver, Colorado. He was born on April 2, 1992 in Midland, Texas to Daniel Gordon and Kerri Dawn (Bennett) Jensen. Alex was very active with church activities at Legacy Church where he was a former member, and at the New Hope Christian Church in Wylie where he was a current member. Alex attended Davis Intermediate School in Wylie. He loved to play football and played Defensive End and Running Back for the Wylie Patriots proudly wearing #9, and was also selected for the Wylie Football League All Star Team. Alex also played for the Wylie Magic Basketball Team and enjoyed video games. Alex gave his all in everything he did. He lived life with great enthusiasm and will be extremely missed by all who knew him. He is survived by his parents, Dan and Kerri Jensen of Wylie, Texas; grandparents, Bruce and Cheryl Jensen of Plano and Gene and Janice Bennett of Riverton, Kansas; great grandparents, Irvin and Gladys Bennett of Clinton, Missouri and Winnie Anderson of Plano; sister, Beth Jensen of Wylie; dog, Lucky; aunt and uncles, Kevyn and Cynthia Bennett of Allen, Texas and James Jensen of Overland Park, Kansas. A memorial service will be held at 3:00 p.m. Monday, January 3, 2005, at Legacy Church, 4501 Legacy Drive in Plano with Pastor Gene Wilkes and Pastor Keith Spurgeon officiating. The family request casual dress for the memorial service. Wylie residents are invited to wear Pirate spirit attire. The family invites you to visit www.liveaudiomix.com to share your thoughts about Alex. In lieu of flowers, donations may be made to the Alex Jensen Memorial through the Wylie Football League at any location of the American National Bank of Texas.

" *Alex and I were friends, I met him through Beth, he was nice and i will miss him a lot.* "

Alexis Rose Washington, January 3, 2005

My heart was broken and I was devastated for the family. I was in shock thinking *how could this happen to such wonderful Christians?* I wanted to do anything I could to help, but did not have a clue what could ease the pain of this tragic loss. As humans we base our expectations on our own experiences, so I was so concerned for the family thinking that Dan and Kerri would become alcoholics, neglect Beth, and spiral out of control because that is what happened to my family when my brother died. Although I couldn't identify with the loss of a child, I could identify with loss, so I reached out to Kerri and we had coffee. As we talked, I was amazed at her strength, the hope within her, and how she could just talk about Alex. (The way I had learned to cope with the loss of a loved one was to pretend they never existed, never say their names or talk about them, so for her to share openly about her son whom she just lost was surreal for me.) Looking at her, I told her that her strength is amazing. I will never forget her looking into my eyes and saying "My strength comes from the Lord." I left that day in awe of the whole situation, thinking maybe my family should start going to church. That day a seed was planted in my heart by God through Kerri Jensen. Ultimately it was through Alex Jensen, whose death, though so tragic, has brought so many to the Lord including me.

Not long after my visit with Kerri, God started really moving in my life. Looking back, there were also a lot of spiritual forces trying to stop this movement and derail me. Alexis, Sammy, and Warner started going to church regularly, but Hailey and I both worked at Dickey's on Sunday mornings, so we could not attend. It felt good that my younger kids and husband were going; and I didn't really think I needed to attend. It was also during this same time that my husband relapsed on Meth. He always came home right after work, but one night he didn't. After many hours of waiting, his car finally pulled up to the trailer. When he stepped out of the car and I could see his face, I knew. He could never hide his drug use from me because I could tell by the way he set his mouth. I was devastated and didn't know what to do. He said a girl he worked with offered it to him and he just did a line, but he promised never to do it again. Thinking my only choice was to believe him, I did, but this started a cycle of drug use that lasted for four years, that I let go on way too long. Not long after Warner's relapse, I received a call from him while I was at work. Our oldest daughter Hailey had been caught at school with Xanax and although she was not going to be arrested, she was being charged. Warner could not go to the school because he was high on Meth, so I had to go pick her up. I was so scared for her. My main fear was the cycle of addiction that ran in our family and what to do to stop that. She was a wreck when I picked her up, and kept telling me she wanted to die. Well I was not going to take suicide threats lightly, so I took her to Green Oaks to have her admitted and assessed at the same place I had sent my father a few months before. She stayed for the night; and that gave me time to think about what to do.

Feeling hopeless and alone because Warner was on a Meth binge, I called the pastor of the church. Now remember I had not attended the church yet and really did not know Keith. I told him that my family needed to meet with him, that we had a lot going on. The next week my kids and I went to see Keith Spurgin, the pastor of New Hope Christian Church in Wylie. I will never forget walking into his office and sitting down. Warner did not go because of his drug use and I didn't mention that because I was pretending it wasn't going on and hoping my kids hadn't realized he was using again. It is so hard and tiring to keep destructive secrets. He looked at all of us and asked how he could help. I then unloaded and said I needed help with my kids. Hailey was in a lot of trouble because of possession of drugs at school and the other two fought a lot and that we just needed help. He looked me in the eye and said "Susan, we need to take a look at you first, not the kids." I was almost offended because I really thought I had it together, but I was open to listen to him. The kids left his office and he told me I needed to get into relationships with people, preferably Christians. He said there were two ways to do this: either start attending a home team or start attending church on Sunday. His advice was to attend a home team because it was a smaller setting and I could really develop relationships with people. Leaving there that day, I made the decision to ask for Wednesday off to attend a home team. I was very reluctant, thinking if the people in the home team really got to know me, they would reject me and my kids. So I thought *I will attend and just play the part expected of me never having to let them know that I had been to prison; was in recovery; was a felon, etc.* I had been playing various roles my whole life and I thought I could pull it off, but God had a lot more in store for me.

The first night that I attended home team, a man was sharing his testimony. He was a successful man that I had really looked up to. As he shared his story about being sexually abused as a child and put in a mental hospital for a while, I was shocked because you would have never thought that. He had a beautiful wife, great job, and wonderful kids. After hearing his testimony, I felt a little less alone in this world, but I was still not ready to be open. The second time to attend home team came and

Dan Jensen shared this time. He had been to an encounter weekend the week before and God had revealed a lot to him. Dan had been feeling extremely guilty about his son Alex and not spending more time with him. God had shown him that the guilt he was feeling was not from God and he needed to let it go, that the enemy was trying to destroy Dan by using this guilt. As he was speaking, a memory of my mother popped into my mind, the pain on her face when I told her I wished she were dead. I was reminded of all the guilt I felt over her death and it was just too much for me. I was completely broken and I started crying so hard I fell out of my chair. Sobbing, I told this group of people everything about myself, from the death of my mom to my time in prison. It was like a flood gate was open and I was able to release all this pent up pain, sadness, and anger. Exhausted, I looked up after my emotional display and I was surrounded by these wonderful people. For a moment I thought they might have stones in their hands after learning of my wretched past, but all I saw was looks of love and acceptance on their faces. They started hugging me and praying for me; and I just started crying more because I thought they would reject and push me away but they didn't. I know now that it was at that moment Jesus came into my heart; and I know there was rejoicing in Heaven because I finally let the walls I had been building for years be broken down. God's light was everywhere. It was amazing. The only thing I didn't share was Warner's relapse and that was a mistake because that left one wall up; and when we have those walls and secrets, Satan will use it to try and destroy us.

After that night I started seeking God with all my heart. I joined a women's Bible study on Friday mornings, attended home team each Wednesday and told Bill I needed Sundays off to attend church. If church was open, I was there. I was desperate for God and His Word, wanting to grow. It was an awesome time as I developed relationships with women, real friendships that are dear to me today. Slowly as these relationships grew, I didn't feel so alone in the world anymore. God is just so faithful, but we have to do our part. We cannot be passive; there are actions we must take. This was a beautiful time. As I met with women on Tuesdays and Fridays, I wanted so much to share with them about my husband's drug use, but I was too scared. The thoughts I had were: they will take your kids and you have already had a CPS case; you can't support your family on a 7.25 an hour job; you are alone in this world and there will be no one to help you. (Since I had no family, the only help we got was from Warner's parents and, at the time, they blamed me for all the trouble we had been in. They were also not aware of his relapse.) The fear was paralyzing; and I just couldn't be honest about it. Thinking back, I had just had this huge spiritual experience by being honest and getting everything out about my past, but this area was still a stronghold that had me trapped. The fear blinded me when I had just seen how the truth had set me free. It is just as obvious as I look back, but I certainly did not see it then.

As I got closer to God, He really started speaking to me where I could understand; and He also began testing me. The first test that I remember happened at Dickey's. By this time, I had been promoted to manager and was running the store when Bill was out. One Sunday, I was in charge and a man called the store saying we had messed up his order by giving him the wrong meat. I asked where he lived and told him I would deliver the right order as soon as possible; and apologized for the mistake. He was very nice; and said he would also like to buy a turkey sandwich. After hanging up, I thought, *I will just give him the sandwich because we had made a mistake and hopefully that would make up for it.* We prepared the order and I drove over to the man's home. When I arrived and knocked on the door, everything was very chaotic. There were a lot of people, little kids, and pets. He cracked open the door, trying to not let his dog out, and he was holding a baby. I handed him his order. He handed me five dollars for the turkey sandwich and shut his door. Looking at the money, a battle started in my mind. My first thought was that I had planned on giving him the sandwich and I needed to try and give his money back, but then I thought I will just keep this five dollars as a tip. Thoughts like this continued as I drove back to Dickey's: *I deserve this $5 because I drove my own car and used my own gas,* to a thought that said; *he didn't intend for that money to be a tip, he thought he was buying a sandwich and he might not want to tip you since you had messed up his order.* I was getting really tired of the conflict in my mind, but the bottom line was I wanted to justify stealing that money. I could have called Bill and told him the situation and asked what to do with the five dollar bill, but I didn't want to. I could have returned to the home and asked the man himself, but for some reason, I desperately wanted that money. Arriving back at Dickey's, I said to myself, *I don't want to think about this now, I will put the money in my pocket and deal with it later.* So I folded the bill and slipped it into the back pocket of my jeans.

The restaurant was very slow, so I just went and stood in the To Go section, trying not to think, but God was not going to let this stop. As I looked around the restaurant, a memory from prison surfaced in my mind, that first night that I spent in Woodman. ... I woke up, looked around and said to myself, "How on earth did I end up here? Where did it go so terribly wrong?" God spoke clearly then and said, "It was situations like this that got you to prison. Small compromises in seemingly innocent situations that are not black and white." He showed me if I kept the money, next time I wouldn't think twice about it. Then it would be easy not to ring someone up and pocket the cash, which could lead to me taking cash out of the register. He showed me how I made small compromises from a girl who did not, would not do drugs, until I became a full blown drug addict.

It was a terrifying vision, but so clear to me. I ran to the cash register and rang up the turkey sandwich, putting the five dollars in the drawer. It was such a powerful experience and really showed me that the little things are very important. Song of Solomon 2:15 (GOD'S WORD Translation) "Catch the foxes for us, the little foxes that ruin vineyards. Our vineyards are blooming." From that point forward, I was very guarded and anytime I start to justify something (if only in my mind), I knew that I had been given a warning from God; and I really need to pray and seek His guidance. It is a slow fade when we self-destruct, so beware of those small foxes in your life wherever they may be!

CHAPTER 9
Beautiful People Do Not Just Happen

The most beautiful people we have known are those who have known defeat, known suffering, known struggle, known loss, and have found their way out of the depths. These persons have an appreciation, sensitivity, and an understanding of life that fills them with compassion, gentleness, and a deep loving concern. Beautiful people do not just happen."
— Elisabeth Kübler-Ross

The spiritual growth in my life was awesome but living with an addict was not. The kids now knew Warner was using because he was again a full blown addict. Meth addiction is horrible. His drug use caused a lot of strain on our family, but I was still hoping he would quit, scared to tell anyone for fear I could not make it on my own.

I was desperately trying to find a second job to supplement my income, but was not having any success. I still loved Dickey's, but I really needed to make more money to support my family. Warner had gotten fired from Albertson's and was working for a moving company. This was probably a better job, but a lot of money was going to dope. One day in the Wylie paper I saw an ad for a tutor and made the call. The man was very nice, was just starting this tutoring business and wanted to meet me. This was very exciting and right up my alley, because I had been a teacher. A tutoring job and my Dickey's job might be enough for me to support the family by myself and not have to rely on Warner. We decided to meet at Starbucks. During the drive over there, I began to get nervous. This would be the first time that I had to say I had felony drug convictions, because I knew it would come up, and I hadn't filled out any paper work. The battle began and negative thoughts were bombarding my mind. "Only say what you have to," "if he doesn't ask don't tell," "keep it a secret then you can get the job and maybe he won't find out." I was trying to argue with myself in my head, but it was very tiring. Arriving at Starbuck's, I got out of my car and walked into the store. The second I walked in, I looked over to a couch and saw our youth pastor at the time working on a lap top. He did not even notice me. To be honest, I don't even know if he knew who I was, but I knew him and he represented truth and light to me. I knew then I had to be honest because I believed this was no coincidence, and God had put Bret in my path that day to keep me honest. I sat down for my interview; and it went very well. He was thrilled I had been a teacher and had a special education degree. He was about to offer me a job when I said I need to share something with him; and he nodded. Then I proceeded to tell him about my drug addiction and convictions. He was so very kind to me and told me that he would love for me to work for him. He really liked me as a person, but he could not hire me because he wouldn't be able to insure me as I went into people's homes. This was a powerful day in my life because it was the first time I really had to verbally talk about my past, knowing I might be rejected. But he didn't reject me, *Susan;* he just couldn't overlook the felonies. There is a huge difference and it became clear that day. I left feeling on cloud nine because I had been obedient, overcame my fear and although I didn't get the job, I wasn't rejected. It was a beautiful day and a lot of healing took place.

The only problem was I still needed a second job or a better paying job. God again had a good plan for me that was about to take place. One day, I was working at the drive thru and a beautiful girl pulled up. She was a regular customer; and you could tell she was very successful. We would talk through the window and laugh. I really liked her. Out of the blue that day, she told me she wanted to hire me to be her personal assistant. I was in shock and asked what she did. She told me she was a sales counselor for Highland Homes; and I would assist her in selling new homes. This sounded very exciting, but I had to tell her about my past. I told her I would love to consider it, but needed to talk to her and tell her some things. She assured me I didn't and that I would be perfect for the job; but I insisted.

We made an appointment to meet. I was very excited. As I was driving to the model home on the day of the appointment, the battle started in my mind. Yes, again, my mind is a war zone with thoughts like, *I don't need to tell her everything; She said she didn't need to know anything else, and She said I was perfect for the job!* As I was trying to talk myself out of being up front and honest, I looked over and saw our youth pastor jogging down the street. I could not believe it. It was just like

God always put Bret in my path during these tests to remind me to be honest. Just the sight of him stopped the battle in my mind and I knew I had to tell the truth. I met with Shannon and told her about my past. It was so hard for me, but she looked up in my eyes and told me it didn't matter, she still wanted to hire me. She then touched my arm tenderly and told me she was sorry I had such a tough life. I left that day with a new job!

At this time the trailer was falling apart and our landlord would not fix what was broken. For instance the AC went out in the summer and it was a week or so before he did anything. The heat was unbearable. There was a woman — Jill Crowe, an angel from the Lord — in my Bible study who came to me one day and told me she had a house that she would rent to me. It was a cute, older home and she was going to lower it below the rent we paid in the trailer. This was such a blessing from God; and I know that God put Jill Crowe in my life. She is a true servant of God and is so kind and generous. I can honestly say, I don't know where I would be if she weren't in my life. I love her with all my heart and am so grateful for her.

This move ended up being a new beginning and a lot of things were about to change. Hailey was a senior at this time, Alexis a freshman, and Sammy was in eighth grade. Warner's drug use was out of control and I made him leave, but I would let him come back at times because I felt sorry for him. He still helped me with the bills, but I could not have him in my home all the time. The rest of the family was doing okay, although there was a lot of conflict with Hailey and Alexis. One day they got in a huge fight and Hailey decided to move into a friend's home. I was very sad, but didn't know what to do. My children bore the brunt of our drug use from the neglect they received as young children, to the chaos in the home and this just intensified with Warner's relapse and subsequent use that I allowed to continue. My hopes were to have a stable secure home for the kids, but that was not the case. Even though I was failing in that area, I was still seeking the Lord with all my heart. I am so grateful to God that I did not relapse with dope in the house. It is truly a miracle; and it just confirms that God had delivered me from that addiction. Because I was an addict, a full-blown addict, and it was not pretty or glamorous in anyway. And although I have had a somewhat tough life, I could have made better choices and I didn't. So I am accountable for all my bad choices, but I am just so grateful that God delivered me from it. I have not seen many people get off Meth.

This time of my life was very hard, but it was also very rewarding and I continued to develop my relationship with God and others. God is always in control; and there was about to be a huge blow-up that ended up being the best thing that could happen. Remember I was being obedient in many areas of my life, but I was still hiding Warner's drug use, and that was eating away at all of us; and certainly not setting a good example for my kids. God was about to throw a brick in my window to get my attention. One Wednesday night, as I was on my way to home team, I called Alexis and she told me she was going to her boyfriend's house. I told her she couldn't go and she responded that she would do whatever she wanted. Not sure how to handle this defiance, I drove to her boyfriend's home to retrieve her cell phone that I paid for. We got into an altercation and she punched me in the eye, causing me to bleed. Shocked by this, I called the police and had her arrested. She cried, begging me to not let them take her, but I was exhausted and knew I needed time to think. Also, as a former prisoner, I knew jail was not that bad. It got my attention, so I let them take her. She stayed there two weeks.

After Alexis was arrested, some women from my home team came over reassuring me that I had done the right thing. At this moment, Warner walked in so high on Meth, I lost it. I told him he had to get out of the house and he was not welcome there anymore. I threatened to have him arrested and call his probation officer if he ever stepped foot in there again. He left embarrassed, since women from the church were there, but I didn't care. I then told them about his relapse; it was so freeing. This was a huge lesson. I hid his addiction for three years. It almost destroyed all of us. I had a lot of accountability in that situation. I let my kids and myself down, but I drew a line in the sand that night. God finally got me to speak out that dark secret and healing began to take place.

Not long after the Wednesday night blow-up, I was informed that Warner was going to a six month rehab in Mabank. This was great news; and I wished the best for him. My job was going well. I had just gotten a new boss who had two communities, so I was allowed to work as much as I wanted. For six months I worked seven days a week, 9-10 hours a day. It was the only way I could make it and support my family. It was not the best solution, but I didn't know what else to do. Hailey came back home at this time and Alexis got out of Juvenile Detention, so I was with all my children. We took Alexis to the doctor and had her assessed. The diagnosis came back depression and she was put on medication. Finally there was calm after the storm we had been living for the last three years. Warner was doing well in rehab and I supported him throughout this time. I wasn't sure what to do about my marriage; I was so very tired of it all. One night I got down on my knees and prayed to God for a sign to tell me if I was supposed to leave and get a divorce or try to work out our problems. My answer came the next day in the mail. As I opened the mailbox, I saw a letter from my mother-in-law. This was weird because she lives one street over from us, so we don't usually get mail from her. Opening the letter, I realized it was a copy of mine and Warner's wedding announcement from the Stephenville paper from years ago. As I read the announcement, I remembered that day and the hopes and dreams we had for our life together. None of those had come true, but I knew that was my answer from God, to work on my marriage, so I was obedient.

New home sales were a lot of fun; and we were doing well. As time went by, I was learning the business and felt more comfortable with my job, but I had still not sold anything on my own; and that was what I was hoping to do. This would prove to myself that I could take someone through a sale and close the deal. One Wednesday, a day I always work alone, a girl came in looking for a home for her parents. She needed something that could close fast in the $275,000 range. We had the perfect home sitting on the ground. It was listed at $314,000, but I knew we needed to move it and what incentive I had to offer. We walked the home, and she was very excited, thinking her parents would love it. Later, she brought them to see it and they were also very interested in the home. It was time to negotiate the deal. The buyer's name was Alicia and she had a list of changes she wanted to make. She had made an offer of $272,000 including the changes. I was getting very excited because I knew I could make this work, unless she had some unrealistic change that cost a lot of money. She started going down her list and my excitement grew, she really only wanted to repaint some rooms, change the cooktop to gas, and put some crown molding in a room. This was going to be the first home I sold all by myself. I was thrilled.

As we were talking about paint colors, a thought popped into my head, telling me to tell her about myself. I just shook away the thought and continued to talk paint. A little later, the thought came back and it was much more specific, saying "Tell her about being a teacher, Meth addict, prison, etc." Knowing this could not be from the Lord, I started rebuking Satan in my head, telling him to get away from me in the name of Jesus. The thoughts would not stop. This prompt from the Holy Spirit got stronger and stronger. I could not concentrate and my mouth went dry. All I knew was that I had to tell; I just had to be obedient. Every sensation was so strong. I didn't even know where to interject this; we had not had a personal conversation at all, but I knew I had to. Alicia said she would like to paint the kitchen a color called Autumn Tan. I marked it down and then I just said, "I want to tell you a few things about myself; before I came to work here I was a teacher but then I got addicted to Meth and was sent to prison, but now I am clean." My eyes were downcast as I told her this, thinking I was probably going to lose my first sale by telling my potential buyer I was an ex-con and felon.

Slowly I raised my eyes up and looked into her face. There were tears streaming down her cheeks. Crying, she told me she had a younger brother who was college educated and had been an executive at Dell Computer, but he got addicted to Meth and had lost his job and home. She also told me she was a probation officer and had worked as a counselor in a Substance Abuse Prison Facility and she had never seen anyone get off Meth successfully. She thought God must have sent me that day to give her hope about her brother! I could not believe how God worked that day through me; and I almost blew it with my selfishness and greed. Alicia did buy the home that day and we are good friends still. At the time, I thought God would use me as an instrument to save Alicia's brother, but that hasn't happened . ….yet! You never know the plans of God. This was one of the most powerful experiences I have ever had. God will use us, but we have to be obedient and say, "Here I am, send me" or he will send someone else. Don't miss your moment because you are afraid. God will get you through it! I was so incredibly blessed that day spiritually, emotionally, and even financially! God is so awesome!!!

As I think back to this time, it is strange because I was more financially secure than I had been in a long time. My bills were all paid and there was extra money. It was really unbelievable. Now I was working 70 hours a week, but it was still amazing. God was blessing us as Warner was at rehab. Not one time did I have to ask anyone for help. I am still amazed about that. Hailey was about to graduate from High School and I was so proud of her. Our hopes were that Warner would graduate from rehab to watch her walk the stage.

Warner did graduate from rehab to watch Hailey walk across the stage. We were both so proud to see her graduate, but Warner's sobriety did not last. He did not relapse on Meth, but began to drink. I was suspicious by his behavior and then one day, it was obvious. I found empty beer bottles in the trash. I was devastated and did not know what to do. My first instinct was to kick him out, but I was just so very tired and the only way I could make it on my own was to work 70 hours a week; and I just couldn't do that anymore. I told him he could live at the house, but he would sleep on the couch and we would split the bills. We settled into that routine.

Warner's drinking was driving me crazy. I would always check his breath when he came home; and he usually smelled like alcohol. I would check his car and the trash for beer cans or caps, and when I would find them, I would blow up screaming at him to quit. One evening my son, Sammy, said, "Mom, we can handle Dad's drinking a lot better than your reaction to his drinking." Out of the mouths of babes! I looked at him, knowing he was right. I was making everyone miserable by my screaming and yelling over something of which I had no control. I promised to change; and did for the most part. There were times I slipped, but I accepted that I could not change Warner's drinking while I could control my behavior. The drinking did not stop, but our home became a lot more pleasant when I changed my reaction. I had to make a choice and, to be honest, I could not make it on my own financially, so I let my husband share the house with me. I don't know if that was the right decision, but there was no violence or drug use. I made an imaginary line in the sand, knowing what I would not tolerate, and that line has not been crossed. To be honest, if I was financially secure, this situation would have been handled differently. But what I knew in my heart was in spite of the drinking, Warner was a good man with a heart of gold. I have never met anyone with a stronger work ethic. He will help anyone in need no matter what it costs him. I have always admired and respected that about him. I know he loved all of us with all his heart, but his addiction had such a stronghold. I am thankful that, for the most part, I could see him through God's eyes.

We had settled into our routine and life was moving along. Alexis was a sophomore in high school and Sammy was a freshman. Hailey had graduated, was going to school and working full time. Alexis was still with the boyfriend from the year before; and we still had many struggles at home. She assured me she was not having sex. It was at this time I moved into leadership at my church. We have small groups on Wednesday nights which totally transformed my life; and I began training to lead a small group with a recovery theme. I was so excited, embracing this new venture, feeling very humbled that I, a convicted felon and ex-convict, could be in leadership at New Hope. God certainly was, and still is, transforming lives through that church.

As time went on, I was beginning to be a little concerned about Alexis because I knew she had not had her monthly cycle. Our house is a very small one bathroom, so I was quite aware of all the cycles of my girls because, as so often happens, we had synchronized menstrual periods, but Alexis did not. I really didn't say much because she had promised me she was not having sex, but I continued to observe her. I was so relieved when she came into the bathroom and took a bunch of feminine napkins to keep in her purse. It was not long after that, though, that I realized she was not using them. I decided it was time to sit down and talk.

She looked at me, started crying and told me to go buy a pregnancy test. We went to the store, bought one; and gave her the test at home. I was ecstatic at the results because I thought it was negative, but Hailey looked at me incredulously and told me to look again. It did show positive, so I went and bought five more tests. The results were the same; my fifteen year old daughter was pregnant! Of course my first selfish thought was, "What will people think about me?" which led to, "We can go get an abortion and no one will ever know," but that is not who I had become. Alexis wanted to have the baby.

My mind was bombarded with thoughts; and I had my small group that night, so I just pushed them aside. After worship that evening, I spoke up and said I had something to share. I told a group of about twenty that my fifteen year old daughter was pregnant. They surrounded me with love and prayer; and told me of multiple people from our church that had experienced the same thing. I was so blessed because I had felt so alone in this situation, but that was far from the truth. Satan wants to isolate and make us feel alone. I am so glad I didn't allow that and shared, even though I was scared. This situation has always made me reflect on how many people suffer in silence because they feel shame, when God's healing light would bring comfort and let you know you are not alone. Everyone has something going on; and you can usually identify with others problems. That is why God has developed us for relationships. God created us for relationships so we can speak into each other's lives and be a support to each other as we experience similar trials. "Who comforts us in all our troubles, so that we can comfort those in any trouble with the comfort we ourselves receive from God." -*2 Corinthians 1:4 NIV*

After that night at the home team, Alexis and I discussed the options for her pregnancy. She could keep the baby or put the baby up for adoption. After a lot of thought, Alexis decided to keep her baby. Alexis had to sign up for Medicaid because we did not have insurance. After she was accepted, we found a doctor.

Surprisingly, Alexis' pregnancy was a time of healing for our relationship. She was so young; she didn't even have her driver's license, so I was very involved, taking her to each appointment, sonogram, and various tests. It was an exciting time; and we got along better than we ever had. It just seemed that her chemical balance at this time was calming to her. It was amazing. She took wonderful care of herself. She ate things she would never consider before because it was good for the baby. She read out loud because she heard babies could hear in the womb. She also would put headphones on her stomach and play Beethoven and Mozart because she heard that was good for the baby. Alexis and the baby would share a room, so we got Alexis a single bed and a crib. Warner painted the room a beautiful yellow; and it was just perfect. We were so excited about the arrival of Riley Nicole. We had learned she was having a little girl. One of my very good friends held a baby shower for Alexis and so many people came! It was a beautiful day. Alexis would go to youth each Wednesday Night and was accepted; no one shunned her because she was pregnant. That is what I loved about New Hope. The people just loved us and accepted us. Finally on June 25, 2008, Riley Nicole was born. Hailey (Alexis' sister) and I were in the delivery room. It was such an amazing moment watching the birth of my first grandchild.

It was a beautiful summer; and Alexis was such a good young mother. She nursed Riley during those lazy summer days and nights, which passed by as her friends dropped by to visit frequently. As summer turned into fall, I thought Alexis might quit nursing Riley but she was committed to doing what was best for her baby girl. Each morning I would drop her off at school; and she would jump out of my car with a backpack on one arm and breast pump on the other, wave goodbye and run into the building. Those sweet moments are frozen in my mind.

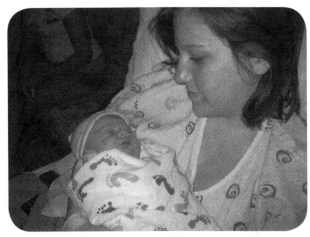
Alexis and baby Riley

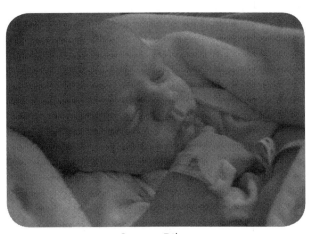
Sweet Riley

CHAPTER 10
Without The Struggle

The Butterfly Would Never, Ever Fly He learned that the butterfly was SUPPOSED to struggle. In fact, the butterfly's struggle to push its way through the tiny opening of the cocoon pushes the fluid out of its body and into its wings. Without the struggle, the butterfly would never, ever fly. The boy's good intentions hurt the butterfly.
–Struggle is Good!

In the fall of 2008, Alexis started her junior year in high school and Riley went to a babysitter. It was a time of calm again, except for Warner's drinking. We all adjusted to a baby in the home and life was good. During this time, God placed it on my heart to begin writing.

The housing market was really struggling during this time; and I learned my hours were to be cut. Wondering how I would survive, I decided to check into getting my teacher certificate reinstated. Not really sure how to go about it, I wrote a letter to TEA and had many of my friends, pastors, employers, etc. write letters on my behalf. Honestly, I didn't think it could happen but on Christmas Eve of 2008, I received a letter from the Texas Education Agency. Holding the letter in my hand, I went back to finish my last few hours at work. I was alone that day, but I couldn't bring myself to open the letter. I was so scared of being disappointed, but finally I gathered the courage. It was the best news I could ever imagine. They had made a decision to reinstate my certificate, if I passed a drug test and stayed out of trouble.

TEXAS EDUCATION AGENCY
1701 North Congress Ave * Austin, Texas 78701-1494 * 512/463-5734 * FAX 512/463-8538 * http://www.tea.state.tx.us

Robert Scott
Commissioner

December 22, 2008

Susan Washington
1020 Mardi Gras Ln.
Wylie, TX 75098-4125

Dear Ms. Washington:

I am in receipt of your request to remove the suspension of your educator's certificate and the numerous letters in support of your request. The decision has been made to lift your suspension upon receipt of a document substantiating that you are drug free and on the condition that you remain free from drug use.

I am delighted to convey this response to you and I look forward to hearing from you.

Very truly yours,

Merle Hoffman Dover
Associate Deputy Counsel
Educator Certification & Standards
512-463-9710

During the fall of 2009, I decided to make some changes in my life. God was working through me, but I felt stuck in a way. Warner was still drinking. I was extremely overweight and could not get a handle on it. It was like I had replaced a few addictions (alcohol, drugs, and tobacco) for a food addiction. . at least it was legal. One night I had a dream that my blood pressure was 2000/1000 and I woke up in a sweat. To be honest, I didn't really know what my blood pressure was; I had not been to the doctor in a while because we didn't have insurance or the money. But I was scared enough and had some savings set aside that I decided to get a comprehensive physical. Surprisingly, I was completely healthy. Although I was overweight, my cholesterol was a little high, blood pressure fine, and all my blood work came back in the normal range. I had feared such bad results, thinking I was probably pre-diabetic or much worse, that a blanket of peace fell upon me. I made the decision to lose weight; and really do it this time! I finally *said enough is enough!*

Me at 216 pounds

A friend of mine from church had done a program called *Slim 4 Life,* had lost almost 100 pounds and kept it off. After much prayer and consultation with Warner, I decided to do the program. It was very expensive, probably over $1000 in all, but I made the decision to borrow the money from my 401k to start. It had been so long since I had been thin; to be honest, I couldn't even imagine it. When I was on Meth, I was not thin. I was probably the only fat Meth addict in the world. I remember sitting in the Rockwall County Jail in so much trouble thinking, "I am in all this serious legal trouble addicted to Meth and I am not even skinny." It was quite depressing. I took off weight when I was in rehab, but gained it back in prison. After I was released and quit smoking, I just slowly kept adding pounds.

On December 3rd I started the program and had my mind set to do it! This was a huge investment for someone as financially strapped as me, so that was another driving force. It was also around this time that I got on Facebook and began connecting with old friends. Many of my high school friends probably knew what had happened to me because of the article in the Dallas Morning News; and news like that just seems to spread fast. I decided to be proactive and address the issue of my criminal background when I connected with someone. I typed a summary of my story and sent it to the people I felt prompted to share with. Their reactions were so nice and supportive; I didn't have one unkind comment. After connecting with a guy from junior high school, he told me about a ministry that he was a videographer for. It was a prison ministry and he thought I would be great working for them. This was the best news I had heard in a long time;and I felt the call of God on my life like never before. Jumping into the ministry was one of the best decisions I have ever made; and I began serving in the prison weekly.

The prison was Dawson State Jail in downtown Dallas. I had spent part of my time there so this was very meaningful to me. Connecting with the female inmates and ministering to them was life giving, that is the only way I can describe it. In Isaiah 58:9 "Then you shall call, and the LORD will answer; You shall cry, and He will say, 'Here I am.' " If you take away the yoke from your midst, The pointing of the finger, and speaking wickedness." 10: "If you extend your soul to the hungry, And satisfy the afflicted soul, Then your light shall dawn in the darkness, And your darkness shall be as the noonday." And this is what happened in my life, my light began to shine for the Lord.

The weight began to fall off of me at a steady pace and I began to feel more comfortable about the way I looked. Seed Sowers asked me to be their public speaker when needed; and I embraced that opportunity with an energy and zeal that I didn't know I possessed! It was so obvious that this was God working through me because I was not gifted in the area of public speaking, but when I got up in front of a crowd, whether it was inmates, students, or successful high powered citizens, God took away my fear and would speak through me, sharing my story of his loving redemption. Because when it is all said and done, my story is what HE has accomplished in my life through me, all I had to say was. . here I am, use me Lord!

It was during this time that the Lord also brought healing to my relationship with my father that had become very strained. He was living in a nursing home on Medicaid because he had lost everything to his alcoholism. He was bitter and angry much of the time and, as I always had been, I became the target for his pain. Before I began to lose weight, he would ridicule me saying, "Why did you get so fat? You look awful!" "Take those stupid glasses off." His remarks cut like a knife because I had spent the majority of my life trying to make him love me, trying to make him proud, longing to hear the words, "I love you Susan." But those words never came. Bitterness and anger began to rise within me. I resented him, so I quit visiting, only showing up every now and then. I felt justified in my neglect, remembering how he had neglected and abandoned me, but my self-righteousness and justification didn't quench the conviction I felt from the Holy Spirit. I hate feeling bitter, so I went for counseling.

It was the best decision that I ever made. After a few sessions, the bitterness began to dissipate. My counselor suggested I do a proxy session with someone sitting in as my father; and I agreed, although I didn't think it would work. My requirement was to make a list of all my hurts and what I believed my father should apologize for. My list was long. The morning of the session, I was nervous and still had my doubts, but I drove to the church and sat in Lynn's office. New Hope's Children's Pastor was sitting in as my father. His name was Alan. He is younger than me so I was still very cynical about the whole idea, until we started. Lynn prayed and I released all my pain, sorrow, disappointments, and hurt "to my father," crying from deep within my soul, begging him to just accept me. We all were crying and "my father," in tears, told me he resented me because I was so much stronger than him. He ran but I stayed and took care of mother until her death. He could barely face himself and felt more shame when he looked at me. It was powerful and truth revealing.

That day, I truly forgave and accepted my father for who he was, not expecting any more than he could give. I left the church and drove straight to the nursing home. When I entered his room, he smiled a little asking me where I had been and why I had not been to see him. Shrugging, I told him I would be there from now on. Then I kissed him on his forehead, telling him I loved him. He scoffed, as he always did with any form of affection, and we watched television in silence.

A few months later, he got terribly ill; and I was worried about his salvation. Although I was still intimidated by him, I made the decision to try and talk to him about Jesus one more time. As I entered his hospital room, I told him I needed to talk to him. He growled, but I didn't waver. In one breath, I told him he was forgiven; that I forgave him and that God forgave him. He just looked at me. Then I told him, " I know you did the best that you could, but you just never got over David's death." When I said my brother's name, he broke and the tears began to flow. The walls that had been built up since 1971 came down and he accepted Jesus Christ as his Savior. It was October 9th 2010. He would die a couple months later on December 13th 2010. I was with him when he died. I watched him pass and prayed Psalm 23 and Psalm 91 over him. With his death, my family was gone. It was only me and my children. I was the top of the family tree. As I left the hospital, saddened by his passing, I also felt some relief because I believed he would be the last to die. I didn't have to worry about death anymore and I was so thankful he was saved.

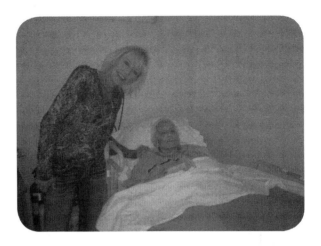

Me and Daddy right before he died

After daddy died, I continued serving with Seed Sowers for over a year and a half. After speaking at their annual banquet, one of my best friends posted a video on Facebook of me sharing my testimony there. The outpouring of loving support from all my friends was incredible and inspiring. After that, I was asked to speak at some of my friends Sunday school classes. God's story in my life was spreading and I loved sharing HIS hope, whether it was in a school, jail, rehab, or church. HE was opening doors for me to share.

The call God had on my life was becoming quite clear at the end of 2010 and into 2011, but my marriage was falling apart. My husband would not make any attempts to quit drinking; and I would get so very angry about it. At times I felt as if my soul was dying. It was painful, but the anger and bitterness began to rise within me. I knew I had to make a change. On Mother's Day in 2011, as a woman shared at church, I felt the Lord speak to me. My pastor Keith Spurgin made a statement, "Sometimes you have to let go and move forward so you can forgive." It was said in response to the woman sharing about her dysfunctional relationship with her mother, but in that moment it was as if God's light was shining only on Keith and me. It was as if the words were directed at me alone and I heard God say, "Susan you need to leave." It didn't make sense, but I received more confirmation as a place for me to live opened up. After my son Sammy graduated from high school, I made the decision to separate from my husband. I moved in with my friend Melanie on August 1, 2011. It was a hard move, but my children were now adults and if I didn't take care of me in this area, I felt as if I would die. I wouldn't be good for anyone. The despondency I felt reminded me of years before, when I made the choice to numb myself. I had to get out and the move was positive for me, at least. A peace washed over me and more healing took place. It was like it was a sabbatical for me to refresh. I didn't do anything differently, but I began to write more and my soul and spirit were renewed.

It was about at this time in 2011 that God placed it on my heart to write my story into a book and the words began to flow. It was quite cathartic to share my life; it helped to further process the pain, and through that process, more healing took place. In the fall of 2011, I learned that a dear friend of mine, Kristie Smith, who wrote a guest column for the Dallas Morning News was going to write an article about my story, sharing the redemption and restoration. As the publication of the article grew near, I knew God had a plan for me to become a speaker and that I needed to capitalize on any publicity I would receive. So through my friend Kurt, we developed a website call *From Pompoms to Prison* where I blogged and people could contact me to speak. We rolled out my website on December 19, 2011, my 51st birthday and it was a success. Kristie's article appeared in the Dallas Morning News on January 21, 2012 and the floodgates were opened.

Kristie Smith: God never gave up on one fallen educator

Published: 20 January 2012 10:02 AM

Related

Kristie Smith teaches visually impaired students of all ages in the Mesquite ISD and is a Teacher Voices volunteer columnist.

Discover the Voices in your community with our interactive map

Become a Voices fan on Facebook

Read Teacher Voices columns

Read Student Voices columns

Read Community Voices columns

Check out Bubba Flint's cartoons

The Skyline High School class from 1979 must have been shocked when they read about one of their own in a surreal article in *The Dallas Morning News*. In 2001, *The News* reported that Susan Deface Washington was arrested on drug charges and her children were taken by CPS workers while she was on her way to prison. The paper included a mug shot of a disheveled, unfamiliar Susan — not an always-smiling cheerleader, not the fun-loving girl next door.

The Susan Deface the class of 1979 remembered was a bouncy, blond, pretty, petite girl with large green eyes and an unlimited amount of energy and zest for life. That's when I became friends with her at an SMU cheerleading camp. Susan was head cheerleader and in the honor society. She was popular and drove one of the nicer cars in the school's parking lot.

However, what none of us knew at the time was that Susan was anything but the happy, perky blond at home, where she was often all alone with an inebriated mother.

When Susan was 10, she and her family were waiting eagerly for her brother David to arrive at the lake and bring the fireworks for a Fourth of July celebration. A man who had one of the only phones in the area walked to the pier looking devastated. He bent down and whispered to Susan's mother that her 18-year-old son had shot and killed himself in his bedroom while the family was away. Susan watched as her mother was carried off the pier.

Susan's parents, besieged by grief, turned to alcohol, soon separated and left young Susan in charge of managing a household and taking care of her intoxicated mother.

Other traumas soon followed: After being named on the honor roll at Skyline's graduation in 1979, Susan found herself with no one in the audience cheering for her. Angry, she went home and lashed out at her mother, screaming that she wished her mother were dead. The following morning, Susan found her mother's lifeless body; her mother was only 49 years old when she drank herself to death on that Memorial Day.

Without The Struggle, The Butterfly Would Never, Ever Fly | 147

Susan turned to her sister, Kathy, who was Susan's rock. Once again tragedy struck Susan's already fragile life. In 1999, Kathy died from cancer, at the same age and on the same holiday as Susan's mother.

Hopeless to be rid of the pain, Susan's years of casual drug use gave way to something darker. The drugs began to take over her career as a special education coordinator, her role as a mother and eventually her freedom.

Finally, Susan woke up one day wondering how she could have gone from her school to rehab to prison in one year's time. One year she was teaching life skills and the following she was in prison, working on a pig farm.

Although others gave up on Susan, God did not.

In 2003, after being paroled, Susan's conversion began when she met a family who lost their child to a tragic accident. They, Susan observed, had not fallen apart but had turned to God and allowed his mercy and strength to help them through. Susan from that day forward surrendered her life to Jesus Christ.

Susan is now an active speaker and author in North Texas, sharing her message in prisons, schools, churches and many other places: There is hope; no matter what you do, how low you go, or how hopeless life seems, God can bring restoration and complete healing.

The Skyline High School class of '79 has every right to be proud of their once bouncy cheerleader who went from pompoms to prison and back home again.

Kristie Smith teaches visually impaired students of all ages in the Mesquite ISD and is a Teacher Voices volunteer columnist. Her email address is ksmith05@me.com. To learn more about Susan's story, visit www.pomponstoprison.com.

Invitations for me to speak came through my website and more articles were written sharing God's work in my life. Dr. Gene Getz asked me to be on his syndicated radio show called *Renewal Radio*. *The Wylie News and Neighbors God* featured articles as well. My dream was unfolding at such a fast rate. Then I was blessed to learn that an agent from the east coast was interested in representing me in the publication of my book. With help from a dear friend, I began working on my book proposal; and in my spare time, I was booking speaking engagements. Life was good and I spent time with my children and grandchildren. On March 5 of 2012 my second grandchild,

Kendall Grace, was born. Ironically, she was born on the same day that my very first boyfriend died at the young age of 52. Alcohol is as evil as drugs, killing people right and left. His death made me so much more thankful for my sobriety. It was bittersweet remembering my young love, but I was more driven to share with the world there is hope, there can be deliverance from drugs and alcohol; and the chains can be broken. My life was living proof.

Mother's Day came and my children and I went to Cheddars in Allen to celebrate. My small family was growing. It was a special time celebrating one old mother (me) and my two young daughters (Alexis and Hailey) who had become incredible mothers. I felt incredibly blessed as I looked at my family, knowing what we had overcome; knowing we had beaten the odds.

Mother's Day dinner 2012 at Cheddars with my children and grandchildren.

Then came Memorial Day, which was a day of death and sorrow for me in the past; and because of that, I always have irrational fears, but I wanted to change that. Melanie and I planned a celebration for our families at her pool. We cooked out and spent the day swimming and making memories. It was a beautiful day of sun, friends, family, and good food. As the day came to an end, and my children left, I thanked God for his blessings in my life. He had truly given me beauty for ashes; and I knew I was blessed. Peacefulness fell upon me as I had hope for what the future held for all of us.

Memorial Day 2012- A day of fun with family and friends. A day I will cherish forever.

Sammy, Alexis, and Riley on Memorial Day 2012

My family: from left to right Tony, Hailey, Warner, Me, Sammy and Alexis holding Riley in front.

My kids: Alexis, Me, Sammy, and Hailey

CHAPTER 11
Mercies in Disguise

What if my greatest disappointments
Or the achings of this life
Is the revealing of a greater thirst
this world can't satisfy
And what if trials of this life
The rain, the storms, the hardest nights
Are Your mercies in disguise
— Laura Story, Blessings

This is where I thought my story would end, feeling secure in my future. I thought I had it all figured out. My plan was to publish my book and continue to share HIS amazing grace through the power of my testimony in any venue that opened up for me. Then on June 7, 2012, I was driving to work and received a phone call that would change my life forever. A phone call where time stood still momentarily; and my life was divided into two parts: before this and after this. There had been many dividing moments like this in my life before, but this would be my greatest test of all.

My 20 year old daughter, Alexis Rose Washington, was killed in an automobile accident while driving to work. As the news that she was gone soaked in, I almost crumbled onto the floor, feeling shame and defeat; but instantly Psalm 139 came into my mind and I raised my tear streaked face, reciting a scripture I had memorized (Psalm 139: 16 *Your eyes saw me before I was put together. And all the days of my life were written in Your book before any of them came to be.*) God reminded me of HIS word. HE knew Alexis would die this day before she was born. I could not have changed that. He did not want me to hold onto the guilt that was so familiar to me. As I felt HIS comforting presence, and HIS living word spoke to me, I felt strong and courageous, knowing I could trust HIM. Knowing HE would bring good from this tragedy; and that I would see her again. I could feel HIS spirit rising within me; it was so very powerful.

From that moment I made a vow to keep moving forward, glorifying God and honoring my sweet daughter. God has met me every step of the way. His glory has met me in my suffering, and I do suffer every day, but He is always there. Many marraiges crumble after the loss of a child; mine was restored as we came together to be there for each other. My life has been full of loss most of which I didn't handle well. I self-destructed, self-medicated, or crumbled, but that is not the case with the loss of Alexis. This has been my greatest loss of all, but through this journey HE has connected me with so many people. He has been right by my side. I have never felt HIS presence so intimately as I have since she passed. What's odd is that I always thought God was going to use Alexis in an amazing way; she was so strong and brave, standing up for what she believed, not concerned about what anyone thought.

Then she died. What is amazing is I was right HE is using Alexis amazingly, like I thought, but it has happened through her death.

I didn't see that coming; life is full of curve balls. There is a lot of pain in this world because this is a broken world and pain will touch all of us in one way or another. And when that darkness invades our lives, we have a choice: we can walk in bitterness and self-pity or we can walk in love and compassion, reaching out to others. For the majority of my life, I took a victim stance, walking in bitterness and self-pity, thinking my life wasn't fair. But because I know God and Jesus as my Savior, I can stand victoriously knowing I am not alone. Through HIM I can see all my blessings. So I have made the choice to walk in love and compassion, reaching out to the hurting and hopeless. My story is about HOPE. ... there is always hope, even in the darkest moments.

In the spring of 2012 before Alexis died, my favorite song was **Blessings** by Laura Story. As I would sing along in my car, I thought the song related to my past but it foreshadowed my future.

Blessings
by Laura Story

We pray for blessings
We pray for peace
Comfort for family, protection while we sleep
We pray for healing, for prosperity
We pray for Your mighty hand to ease our suffering
All the while, You hear each spoken need
Yet love us way too much to give us lesser things

'Cause what if Your blessings come through raindrops
What if Your healing comes through tears
What if a thousand sleepless nights
Are what it takes to know You're near
What if trials of this life are Your mercies in disguise

We pray for wisdom
Your voice to hear
And we cry in anger when we cannot feel You near
We doubt Your goodness, we doubt Your love
As if every promise from Your Word is not enough
All the while, You hear each desperate plea
And long that we have faith to believe

'Cause what if Your blessings come through raindrops
What if Your healing comes through tears
What if a thousand sleepless nights
Are what it takes to know You're near
And what if trials of this life are Your mercies in disguise

When friends betray us
When darkness seems to win
We know that pain reminds this heart
That this is not, this is not our home
It's not our home

'Cause what if Your blessings come through raindrops
What if Your healing comes through tears
And what if a thousand sleepless nights
Are what it takes to know You're near
What if my greatest disappointments
Or the achings of this life
Is the revealing of a greater thirst this world can't satisfy
And what if trials of this life
The rain, the storms, the hardest nights
Are Your mercies in disguise

The words of this song describe my life; and through the trials and pain, I am so thankful I now know the Lord. The storms of life are hard; and storms are inevitable, but they are much worse without the LORD by your side. When you recognize and reach out to HIM, HE will carry you through as HIS word promises.

Isaiah 43:2 When you pass through the waters, I will be with you. When you pass through the rivers, they will not flow over you. When you walk through the fire, you will not be burned. The fire will not destroy you. 3 For I am the Lord your God, the Holy One of Israel, Who saves you.

And that is what HE has been doing since Alexis' death. I have so much to share about this journey, but that is for my next book. When I announced Alexis' death, a dear friend wrote this to me, "I can't begin to understand why you are faced with yet another tragedy, but I know that Satan will do all he can to prevent you from being a beacon for Christ." Then, after Alexis' funeral, a friend sent this message to me, "As I sat in that packed church tonight, I could hear and see God at work in so many who were there. I believe many were saved tonight, Susan. I've never seen that at a funeral before - much less in a regular church service. You guys did so well tonight in sharing your hearts, but Susan you illuminated a God that many in attendance are searching for." Those two messages have stayed with me. They are written on my heart. Many have wondered why I had to go through so much and I believe HE has taken me *From Pom Poms to Prison* . …………………..**So I Can Cheer.** So I can illuminate the God many are searching for cheering them to find their own victory in HIM, as I have found.

God is awesome; and He is using each heartbreak, mistake, and tragedy for HIS glory. Nothing happens in our life without HIS permission. I have had many wonder why I had to endure so much tragedy. I truly believe through each trial HE has strengthened me SO I CAN CHEER. So I can cheer for the hurting, hopeless and weary. SO I CAN CHEER for HIM, shouting out HIS name in praise through the good times and bad. He had taken me *From Pom Poms to Prison*. . SO I CAN CHEER. Because of HIS grace I am still standing, cheering on HIS VICTORY! Please visit my new website to read about upcoming events and my second book in progress. ... *SO I CAN CHEER.*

Made in the USA
Columbia, SC
06 January 2019